Dining in the Garden of Good Eats:

Cooking with "The Book" That Made Savannah Famous

By Deborah & Shane Sullivan

and other NOGS of Savannah

www.midnightinsavannah.com

FATHER & SON
PUBLISHING, INC.
4909 N. Monroe Street
Tallahassee, Florida 32303
http://fatherson.com
800-741-2712

CONTENTS

PREFACE

The most frequently asked question by visitors to Savannah is, "Can you suggest a good place to eat?" The answer is simple. All the restaurants here serve great food! Savannah prides itself on warm hospitality and delectable meals. From home cooked to ethnic cuisine, you cannot make a poor choice!

Growing up in Savannah, I have fond memories of dining at local establishments. On rare occasions when Daddy was not working we would go to Johnny Harris'. The sweet barbeque smells coming from the kitchen filled our senses as we learned our family's stories. Although Daddy has passed, his vivid tales are still echoed at family gatherings as we devour the outstanding barbeque.

Visitors are never strangers at the tables of Mrs. Wilkes's Boarding House. Home cooked dishes are shared with locals and guests. Meals are topped off with her famous cobbler and southern sweet tea. This tradition continues today with lines the length of Jones Street waiting to be seated.

In the fifties, my two maiden aunts, Louise and Marie Saseen opened Southern Kitchen at the corner of Bull and Liberty Streets. Every morning a Rhett Butler look-a-like ate his breakfast at the counter. I overheard my Aunt Marie say that she had been invited to a party at the Mercer Mansion and the gentleman seated on the bar stool had issued the invitation. He was a bachelor by the name of Jim Williams. I was not interested in knowing about Mr. Williams, because I had spotted Gregory Peck in the restaurant. The year was 1962 and the movie, Cape Fear, was being filmed here. Obtaining his autograph was my first priority. Little did I know that Jim Williams would become the subject of a best selling book by John Berendt and movie entitled *Midnight in the Garden of Good and Evil*.

Movie star sightings continue today with stars like Ben Affleck and Sandra Bullock patronizing local restaurants. Likewise, Savannah has a host of her own celebrity chefs like, Julia Child and Paula Deen, owner of The Lady and Sons Restaurant. Paula has placed Savannah on the map with her appearances on The Food Network sharing her famous southern recipes.

I met Deborah Sullivan in the early nineties when she had a gift shop in the basement of the Hamilton Turner Mansion. Nancy Hillis, the character of Mandy in the book, managed the inn upstairs. Here, two local belles charmed tourist with southern accented stories of Joe Odom and other notorious characters from the book.

Deborah, with her husband Shane, now own "The Book" Gift Shop on Gordon Street. With the publication of *Dining in the Garden of Good Eats:Cooking with "The Book" That Made Savannah Famous* readers will be enlightened by a delicious smorgasbord of recipes from Savannah's tastiest eateries and local chefs. Personal favorite family recipes are in abundance. Fans of Mr. Berendt's book will learn trivia and how to throw a "Midnight" themed party.

Dining in the Garden of Good Eats: Cooking with "The Book" That Made Savannah Famous is meant to be perused with a glass of wine, and feet propped up. It is guaranteed to quench your palette and entice you to Savannah, Georgia. Come see us! We will show you where and how to eat.

Sharon Saseen
Artist and Writer

ACKNOWLEDGEMENTS

A big thank you to all the family and friends who donated recipes and/or stories and gave us the help and support we needed when things were not as smooth as we would have wished. To Pamela Lee and Sharon Saseen, two of our most loved artists in Savannah, a special thank you.

Thank you to Hestia of Marblehead, Massachusetts for their unique design of both the front and back covers of this cookbook. As for the restaurants, inns and NOGS of Savannah and the Low Country, we love you and of course could not even imagine this cookbook without you. Thank you, thank you. Much thanks to Herb Traub, Paula, Jamie and Bobbie Deen, Jan Wilson, Karen, Greg and Gary Butch, Norman Heights and Jamie Carver, Donna Balesh, Catherine Moore and Marcy Hill, Rob Bruso, Suzanne Kosic, Cindy Roberts, Marjorie Martin and the Wilkes family, Louise Streed, Dot Gibson, Martha Gibbens Nesbit, Margaret Debolt, Dwayne, Jennifer and Frances, Charlotte Dixon, Brenda and the Savannah Cinnamon family and the Braswell family.

A special thank you to Paula Rogers (Ms. Emma Kelly's daughter) and family, Jack Leigh, The Lady Chablis, Sonny & Cecelia Sciler, Miriam Center, Mary Harty, Joe Odom, Minerva and all the real life characters of Savannah.

Thanks to Dee Dee and Trese for taking care of "The Shop" while we were working on this. Without their help, enthusiasm and dedication, we would not have been able to get this cookbook completed.

A great big thank you to the person who made Midnight come to life and has done unbelievable things for Savannah, John Berendt. Through the inspiration of Bruce Kelly, a friend of John Berendt who suggested he write *Midnight in the Garden of Good and Evil*, not only has "The Book" Gift Shop prospered, but so has most of the Historic District of Savannah. Thank you for working so hard to make this masterpiece. Thank you for your friendship over the years. There is always a special place in our heart for you.

Finally, from Shane to my best friend, Deborah; I have really enjoyed working together with you on designing and gathering information and recipes to make this cookbook a reality. All those late nights while you slept and I typed; well anyway, the next one would be formatted differently. Thank you for being my friend. I love you very much.

ABOUT THE AUTHORS

DEBORAH SULLIVAN

Deborah's family has been in the tourism industry since 1966 and her grandmother introduced her to the business at a very young age. On her road of instruction, one of her first duties was making bank deposits. This introduction into consumer economics instilled a knack of saving money for the proverbial rainy day and gave her an appreciation for watching the ole' bottom line. After learning to manage money, she was then thrust into the Charter Group Division where she got her first working relationship with a real southern gentleman by the name of Joe Odom. Joe often invited Deborah's family into his home where he played the piano for their tour groups while his gracious housekeeper, Gloria, would serve up lemonade. Of course, Joe charmed everyone to the extent where the tour's schedule would be delayed, but it always seemed to work out just fine.

In the early part of the 1990's Deborah opened a small shop on the garden level of The Hamilton-Turner Mansion selling various items from artist in the Savannah area. Then in March of 1994, visitors came to Savannah looking for attractions and souvenirs relating to the landmarks from the movie based on John Berendt's best selling book, *Midnight In The Garden Of Good And Evil*. In those days, there were few souvenirs with this theme so as tourist came to her shop in The Hamilton-Turner House, they seemed delighted to find someone who would talk about the "*Midnight*" book and movie. Deborah remembers spending hours chatting with visitors about Savannah, the city's history and her fellow Savannahians. Most of them wanted merchandise and souvenirs relating to "The Book" which did not exist at that time. So, Deborah went to work designing quality souvenirs and gift items and researching companies about her ideas. Deborah spoke with tour companies about the need of organizing tours centered on the theme and popularity of the "*Midnight*" book. For a while no one seemed interested, but Deborah persevered and now there is a successful "Midnight Tour" and an expanded line of "Midnight" souvenirs and high-end gifts likewise.

Deborah is a member of The Junior League, has worked on The Small Business Counsel, the Chamber of Commerce task force for tourism, was a runner-up for Entrepreneur Of The Year in 1997, and is in Who's Who in Business for 2005. She has been a member and active in support of the Friends of Bonaventure, Friends of the Johnny Mercer Inner City Night Shelter, a teenage runaway home and is a member of Ardsley Park Baptist Church, where she has held many positions.

Deborah has a real love for her family and feels that Savannah is a great place to live. Deborah says, "the older I get, the more charming it becomes." "From living, working, shopping, dining out, and fellowship with others in our beautiful squares, I feel blessed to be a Savannahian and love sharing Savannah with others." From the moment visitors stroll into The Shop, Deborah and her staff become a part of the visitor's vacation memory. "We do whatever we can to make their vacation to Savannah special and cherish the time we can become a part of their wonderful memory."

Not all Savannahians feel the same about The "*Midnight*" Book. When Deborah's shop moved to Calhoun Square at 127 East Gordon Street, things were not so pleasant. "We were welcomed with eggs and tomatoes thrown at our front door and sign." After installing a security system, we discovered the identity of those who were so upset with the "Midnight Madness," and the trouble stopped cold." Now the only problem is the female Ghost who occasionally stirs up mischief inside the shop. Every now and then she indicates her displeasure with where certain items are placed and proceeds to knock them off the table. Not to worry, those items are usually just placed elsewhere and are then not disturbed.

We do hope that everyone who comes to Savannah will fall in love with its' charm and history. We hope that you will enjoy the "Midnight Madness" as much as we do and share the experience with others.

Midnight wishes ya'll
Deborah

SHANE SULLIVAN

When we first spoke of the idea of compiling a cookbook, I took a step back, looked at Deborah and said, "what do you know about cookbooks or cooking for that matter?" "Why, just a few years ago the best thing you made were dinner reservations." All kidding aside, Deborah serves many great dishes which she is delighted to share in this book.

The most meaningful thing for Deb and I is family time. Whether it's birthdays or holidays it is important that these times are shared with our loved ones. Our children's birthdays were always very special and years later, our nieces and nephews still recall Shane, Jr. and Stephanie's birthday parties. Likewise, our families always look forward to the holidays. Everyone who is married knows just how hard it is to split time with each other's families and ours is no exception. Fortunately, both our parents live in Savannah and in close proximity to each other, so we are able to share Thanksgiving with both families. Thanksgiving usually brings us together at the home of my parents Joe and Helen Sullivan. My brothers and sister, with all the grandchildren look forward to these special times shared with their grandparents. After the clean-up, the men gather around the television for the holiday football game while the women catch up on all the girl talk. Then for dinner, we're off to Deb's parents, Don and Nancy Dimick, where we eat dinner with Deb's sister, brother and their families where we can always count on a great time of fellowship with family and other friends as well.

Then, we're off to Atlanta to enjoy a post Thanksgiving dinner with Shane, Jr., his wife Lisa, our daughter Stephanie and their families. We usually enjoy teasing Lisa's parents, Dave and Diane and her younger brother Brian about their "Yankee" heritage, but honestly, they act more "Southern" than some who were born down here and they are good people.

Now, we are making a tradition of going to the mountains of North Carolina, Tennessee or Virginia for the Christmas holidays with the entire Sullivan clan, which is not always an easy task since we need accommodations for a group of 20 or more. Every family member gets the chance to prepare their favorite Christmas fare on these family get-a-ways. Whether it's Belgian waffles, chicken casserole or just beans and franks, we all have fun cooking, eating and just being with family. We love to spend time in the mountains and treasure lots of fond memories of our family holidays. If anyone out there owns rental property in the mountains to host our family or would like to trade homes for the holidays, let me know.

Deborah and I certainly hope you enjoy this cookbook as much as we have enjoyed putting it together. Please share your thoughts and ideas with us. In closing, remember to invest the time to make your own memories with loved ones as it is *never* too late to start.

God Bless!
Shane

ABOUT THE ARTIST

SHARON SASEEN

Romantic paintings of historic Savannah with its flowers and natural landscapes have formed the cornerstone of Ms. Saseen's success. In 1985, she illustrated a print of the Old City Market for the thirtieth anniversary of the Historic Savannah Foundation. In 1987, her prints were featured in a special promotion sponsored by Lord and Taylor entitled "Focus America: Savannah." In 1995 she was honored in a Savannah News Press poll as "Savannah's Best Artist."

Today, she is deeply involved in challenging new projects. Ms. Saseen is proficient in a variety of media, including oil, acrylic, mixed media, and pen and ink. She holds a Bachelor of Fine Arts and Master of Art Education degree from the University of Georgia, as well as a Master of Fine Arts degree from Syracuse University. On art scholarships she studied in Italy, and attended Parson's School of Art and Design in New York City.

Many of Ms. Saseen's most popular works are on display at the signature Gallery and Gallery 209. Additionally, viewing and purchasing may be made by private appointment with the artist.

Sharon Saseen Studios
403 East 46th Street
Savannah, Ga 31405
Phone: (912) 233-1341

THE
RESTAURANTS

River Street East © 2003 Sharon Saseen

AWARD WINNING
AND
LOCAL FAVORITES

BELFORDS

313 West Saint Julian Street
Savannah, Georgia 31401-2401
(912) 233-2626

Belford's is situated in a beautiful old brick building in the heart of Savannah's National Landmark Historic District.

The building is listed in Historic Savannah Foundation's architectural inventory as a notable example of its style and is praised in architectural surveys for its arched windows, exposed brick walls and doorways with semicircular, segmental arched toplights.

The design is attributed to Hyman W. Witcover, a practicing architect in Savannah from 1897 to 1923, who also designed Savannah's City Hall, the Main Library Building on Bull Street and many of the fine residences located in the Chatham Crescent section of Savannah's Ardsley Park. Witcover, a member of the American Institute of Architects, was the first president of the Savannah Society of Architects.

The structure was completed in 1902 for Savannah's Hebrew Congregation. In 1913, the Congregation sold the building to W.T. Belford for $23,000. In the hands of the Belford family, whose early 1900's portrait hangs on the West wall of our main dining room, the building became an important wholesale food company in Savannah. The Belford signs painted on the west side of the building and under the front awning remain to this day, faded by years of weather.

The Belford's Wholesale Food Company was an active and integral part of The City Market, the bustling social and commercial heart of early Savannah. The actual market, a splendid edifice with soaring brick arches and open-air stalls for the sale of produce, fish, meat and baked goods, was located in the area now occupied by the City Market Parking Garage on Ellis Square. The demolition of that market in the late 1950's was a tragedy in the eyes of local preservationists and was the catalyst that began the preservation and restoration movement in Savannah. Ironically, the demolition of the original City Market probably saved four blocks of surrounding feed, seed, grain and produce warehouses —collectively now known as City Market—including the Belford building, now known as Belford's Savannah.

Look around you. The walls carry framed photographs of the area as it appeared during the hey-day of Belford's Wholesale Foods, many of which were provided by the Belford family. There is no experience like it in Savannah ... perhaps, anywhere.

BELFORD'S SPINACH SALAD

3	pounds fresh baby spinach, washed and spun dry
1	large onion
½	teaspoon sugar
6	strips bacon, cut into thin pieces
1	cup sliced mushrooms
1-2	teaspoons clarified butter
4	ounces Bleu cheese salad dressing
6	ounces Bleu cheese, crumbled
6	ounces sugared walnut halves

Peel the onion and slice it into rings. Sauté the onion rings in a small pan with the sugar until they are a light brown color. Fry the bacon until crisp; drain. Sauté the mushrooms in butter until tender. Set the onions, mushrooms and bacon aside, keeping warm.

In a large mixing bowl, toss the spinach and the bleu cheese dressing until the leaves are well-coated. Arrange the spinach onto six chilled salad plates. Garnish with the reserved onion, mushrooms, bacon, crumbled bleu cheese and sugared walnuts. Serve immediately.

Belford's Shrimp and Scallops

½	pound butter
¼	cup peeled carrots, finely diced
¼	cup celery, finely diced
¼	cup red pepper, finely diced
¼	cup onion, finely diced
½	cup flour
1	cup crab stock
1	quart half & half
1	quart heavy cream
1	pound crab claw meat, cleaned
½	cup dry sherry
1	cup Parmesan cheese, shredded
32	large shrimp
32	large scallops
1	tablespoon butter
8	French puff pastry squares
16	ounces fresh baby spinach
2	ounces Old Bay seasoning

First, make the sauce. In a heavy bottom pot over medium low heat, melt the butter. Add the onions, celery, red peppers and carrots and cook until the onions are translucent. Gradually add the flour, stirring well to incorporate it into the butter. This will make a thick roux. Lower the heat and cook the roux gently about 15-20 minutes, stirring often; do not brown. Increase the heat to medium. Gradually add the crab stock, stirring well, and cook until it starts to thicken. Add the half and half, stirring well and cooking until the mixture again begins to thicken. Add the heavy cream and stir well. Reduce the heat to low, cover, and simmer very gently for one hour. Watch it carefully, as it will scorch if allowed to come to a boil. After an hour, add the sherry, the crabmeat and the Parmesan cheese. Warm through and remove from the heat.

Heat the oven to 350 degrees. Bake the puff pastry squares until golden brown. Sauté the shrimp and scallops in the butter until just done. Blanch the spinach in salted boiling water for thirty seconds; remove and drain well.

Arrange the spinach on eight serving plates. Place a puff pastry on each plate; fill each with four shrimp and four scallops. Top with the crab and Parmesan sauce. Garnish the plates with Old Bay seasoning. Serve immediately.

BREAD PUDDING

1	egg
2	cups milk
¼	cup white sugar
¼	cup packed brown sugar
1	stick butter, melted
½	cup pecans (optional)
1	tablespoon nutmeg
1	tablespoon vanilla
1	tablespoon cinnamon
3	cups cubed bread*
1	cup raisins

Preheat oven to 350 degrees. Lightly grease an 8 or 9-inch square baking dish and set aside.

Lightly beat the egg in a large bowl. Add the milk, sugar, butter, cinnamon, nutmeg and vanilla and stir to combine. Add the cubed bread, stirring to coat it well. Allow the bread to soak for at least 10 minutes, stirring once or twice, to ensure it absorbs the liquid mixture.

Stir in the raisins and the pecans (if using). Spread the mixture into the greased baking dish. Bake until firm, or a knife inserted in the middle comes out clean, about 40-45 minutes. Let it cool slightly before serving.

* At Belford's, this is day-old French bread. However, virtually any kind of bread you have on hand may be used for this dish.

CLARY'S CAFÉ

404 Abercorn Street
Savannah, Georgia 31401
(912) 233-0402

Clary's Café, one of Savannah's great little institutions and traditions, tucked into the center of her beautiful Historic District, at the corner of Jones and Abercorn streets. Famous with Savannahians long before "The Book," for over 100 years, Clary's has been a gathering spot for the locals for great food and lively conversations. Dr. Clary had on one side of his store a pharmacy and on the other side of the store a soda fountain and lunch counter. No one could ever come into Clary's without going over to the soda fountain for a vanilla coke, malt, banana split, or ice cream cone. As locals lingered over these treats, you could always count on a lot of laughter and neighborhood gossip.

If you have read *Midnight in the Garden of Good and Evil* by John Berendt, you will know that Clary's was a hangout for so many of the interesting characters that are depicted in this story.

TOMATO BASIL SOUP

2	16 ounce cans diced tomatoes	⅓	cup dry sherry
2	tablespoons fresh basil, chopped	⅓	cup light brown sugar
2	tablespoons oregano	2	cups heavy cream
2 or 3	garlic cloves, mashed and diced		Pinch of salt

Place first 6 ingredients into a 6 quart pot and bring to a boil. Reduce heat and add heavy cream and return to a slow simmer.

FRIED GREEN TOMATOES

2	large firm green tomatoes		Salt and pepper to taste
½	cup flour	4	eggs, beaten
½	cup coarse bread crumbs	1	cup oil

Preheat oil in a large heavy skillet. Slice tomatoes ½ to ¾-inch thick. Dredge in flour. Dip into beaten eggs and coat each side with coarse bread crumbs. Fry until golden brown on each side and serve with Marinara Sauce.

Trivia: What two typical historic features were found in the house of Luther Driggers? (#50)

HOPPLE POPPLE

6	eggs	1	medium white potato,
2	1-inch thick slices of Kosher		cooked
	Salami, cut into ½ cubes	2 or	3 tablespoons butter
¼	cup diced green onion		Salt and pepper to taste
¼	cup diced yellow onion		

Melt butter in a heavy skillet and sauté the onions, peppers, salami and potatoes. Whisk the six eggs together with 2 tablespoons water. Pour eggs into skillet over other ingredients and continue stirring until cooked to desired consistency.

COUNTRY OMELET

6	eggs	2	tablespoons brown sugar
2	tablespoons water	½	cup shredded Cheddar cheese
1	cup apple, peeled, sliced	6	tablespoons butter

Melt 3 tablespoons in skillet and add apples and brown sugar. Cook and stir until tender and remove from skillet (or you can use canned apples). Whisk eggs with 2 tablespoons water. Melt 3 tablespoons butter in skillet and pour in eggs. Let them set on the bottom and then add apples and cheddar cheese down the center of the eggs. Let eggs set a bit more and then fold from outer edge of skillet from left and right side to the center, forming the omelet. Turn omelet over and cook for a minute. Turn omelet over into serving plate.

Trivia: For what invention did Luther Driggers lose a patent? (#4)

VICTORIAN SAUSAGE GRAVY

1 ½	pounds fresh pork sausage	¾	cups flour
1	cup whole milk		Salt and pepper to taste
3	cups heavy cream		

Fry sausage in a large heavy skillet and crumble sausage as it is browning. Add milk, cream, flour and salt and pepper and bring to a slow boil. Slowly add Roux and whisk until thick.

ROUX:

1	stick butter	¾	cups flour
¼	cup retained pork grease from skillet		

Melt butter and pork drippings and slowly add in flour, whisking into a smooth paste.

CHICKEN SALAD

2	cups chicken breast, cooked, diced	¼	cup sweet relish
1	cup mayonnaise	⅓	cup diced celery
¼	cup diced white or yellow onion		Salt and white pepper to taste

Mix all ingredients in a mixing bowl. For extra fancy "company" chicken salad, add ⅓ cup pecan pieces and ½ cup seedless green grapes.

Fun Fact: The rarest edition of *Midnight in the Garden of Good and Evil* is the paper unrevised proofs or the Advance Reader's Edition which the publisher, Random House, sent to the booksellers and reviews in late 1993.

CRAB CAKES

2	pounds lump crab meat	4	eggs
3	tablespoons mayonnaise	1	teaspoon Tabasco
1	onion, diced	⅛	tablespoon cayenne pepper
1	green pepper, diced	1 ½	cups coarse bread crumbs
2	tablespoons diced red pimento		Salt and pepper to taste

Mix mayonnaise, onion, peppers, pimentos, eggs, Tabasco, cayenne, and bread crumbs together thoroughly. Carefully add in crab meat; form crab into 2 ounce patties. Fry in oil at 350 degrees until cakes turn golden brown.

CRAB STEW

2	cups picked crab claw meat	½	cup dry sherry
2	tablespoons melted butter	2	cups whole milk
¾	cup diced celery	1	quart heavy cream
¾	cup diced white or yellow sweet onion	2	tablespoons crab or lobster base
	Salt and white pepper, to taste	¼	cup sweet red peppers, diced
2 or	3 garlic cloves, smashed and diced		

ROUX:

¼	pound (one stick) butter	⅔	cup flour

Melt butter in sauce pan and slowly whisk in flour to make smooth paste.

Melt 2 tablespoons butter in a heavy soup pot and add onions, celery, sweet red peppers and garlic and sauté until tender. Add sherry, milk, heavy cream and salt and pepper and crab base and bring to a slow boil. Add in roux and cook until thick; stir in crab meat.

CLARY'S APPLE BLOSSOM

1	package small flour tortillas (6-inches in diameter)		Vanilla ice cream
1	21 ounce can apple pie apples, warmed	1	19 ounce jar Smucker's Special Recipe Butterscotch Caramel ice cream sauce

You will need to fry tortillas individually into the shape of a taco salad shell. To do this, heat enough oil in a large deep pot, being sure that oil is deep enough to accommodate shell. Place a flat tortilla in hot oil. Using a ladle, immediately press center of tortilla down, holding it until tortilla is set into shape of a shell. Continue to fry until golden brown. Drain each fried shell upside down on paper towels to remove excess oil. Repeat this process for as many servings as you will need, allowing 1 shell per person. This step can be done early in the day.

Just before serving, place a layer of warm apples in bottom of each shell. Scoop ice cream over apples and drizzle caramel sauce over top. Serves 4 to 6.

REAL KEY LIME PIE

1	pre-made graham cracker pie shell, 9 or 10-inch	1	teaspoon cream of tartar
5	egg yolks	6	tablespoons sugar
1	can condensed milk	5	egg whites
½	cup Key West lime juice	1	lime

Mix egg yolks, milk, and lime juice into a bowl. Using a fine grater, grate outer green skin of lime into bowl; retain lime. Mix and pour mixture into pie shell. Bake at 350 degrees for about 45 minutes until firm in center.

After removing pie from oven, let cool. While cooling, beat egg whites in a chilled bowl, slowly adding sugar and cream of tartar, until they form stiff peaks. Cover entire surface of pie with stiff egg whites, sealing at the edges. Return to oven and bake until peaks turn golden brown. Remove from oven and let cool. Slice lime into disks. Cut each disk in half and coat with sugar. Place 8 lime pieces equal distance around top of pie.

Trivia: What did Luther Driggers suggest would be a good cleaning tool for John Berendt's toilet bowl? (#5)

A Savannah Tradition.... Again

301 West Jones Street
Corner of Jones and Jefferson St
Savannah, Georgia 31401
(912) 443-9200
www.crystalbeerparlor.net
crystalbeer1@bellsouth.net

Suzanne Kosic-Owner-Chef

Chef Shirley Carter

Located in the Historical District -2 blocks south of the Civic Center—take Jefferson Street.

Parking is available in their large, well lit lot in the rear of the building. Join us at one of the oldest and best loved restaurants in Savannah. Established in 1933, we proudly serve the best quality of homemade foods, just as they did in the old days.

If you are looking for "THE PLACE" where the locals eat and true Savannah ambience and hospitality, this is it. Just ask any Savannahian about us. Our menu includes: Seafood, fresh ground sirloin burgers, BBQ, Oyster Sandwiches, Shrimp salad, thick cut French fries, thick creamy crab stew, award winning Brunswick stew, seafood gumbo, homemade onion rings and root beer floats for the kid at heart—just to name a few items.

LIVE DIXIELAND JAZZ
Friday nights 7:30-10:30

CRYSTAL BEER PARLOR BRUNSWICK STEW

Chef Shirley Carter

3	gallons of water to boil
2	8 pound boneless pork butts, quartered
1	6 pound hen, split
10	pounds of choice ground beef
3	large potatoes, diced
3	large onions
32	ounces ketchup
32	ounces mustard
64	ounces smoked barbeque sauce
1	#10 can lima beans
1	#10 can corn
3	ounces black pepper
3	ounces of hot sauce
3	tablespoons seasoning salt
	Salt to taste

We do not puree our Brunswick stew at the Crystal Beer Parlor, but leave it chunky and delightful; a true stew at its best.

In a large pot add the 3 gallons of water, bring to a boil. To the boiling water add the pork butts, the chicken and the seasoning salt. Simmer until tender. Once tender, remove from pot, cool and dice into medium bites. Add the 10 pounds of beef to pot, breaking it up as you add it. Return pork and chicken to pot adding remaining ingredients and simmer until potatoes are tender but retain their shape. Feel free to add more hot sauce as you like.

Trivia: Who is the photographer responsible for "The Book" cover? (#49)

Pecan Crusted Drum with Pecan Crab Chutney

Chef Suzanne Kosic

Our Signature dish from our new Gourmet Menu

4 7 ounce Black Drum Fillet (Skin On)
  Pecan Crust
  Pecan Crab Relish
  Lemon Butter Sauce

Pecan Crust:

8	ounces pecans, ground fine
6	ounces flour
3	ounces bread crumbs (unseasoned)
1	teaspoon onion powder
1	teaspoon Creole seasoning
1	teaspoon Old Bay Seasoning

In a food processor, grind all ingredients together until fine. Set aside.

Lemon Butter Sauce:

2	tablespoons butter for sautéing
¼	pound chilled butter (1 stick)
½	cup Chardonnay or any dry white wine
¼	cup Champagne Vinegar
2	Shallots, finely diced
3	lemons, peeled and quartered
½	teaspoon white pepper
½	cup heavy cream
1	tablespoon Worcestershire Sauce (Lea and Perrins)

Using a small sauce pan, sauté shallots and garlic in the 2 tablespoons butter over medium heat until translucent, (3 or 4 minutes). Add white wine, vinegar and Worcestershire, reduce by ¾. While sauce is reducing, add the lemon quarters. Allow lemon to cook for 3 minutes, squeeze out juice by pressing against wall of pan. Remove lemons and continue reduction. Once reduced, add cream and reduce until thick. Whisk in chilled butter a pat at a time whisking continuously until thickened. Add salt and white pepper to taste. Keep warm.

Note for beginners—never fear if for some reason you can not get the sauce thick enough (it takes time to acquire this talent). Thicken with a bit of corn starch mixed in cold wine, add a couple of tablespoons of mixture to sauce at a time allowing sauce time to thicken. Do not add to much corn starch mixture or your sauce will be pasty!

PECAN CRAB CHUTNEY:

8	ounces pecans, coarsely chopped
1	medium onion, finely diced
½	teaspoon garlic, finely diced
1	red bell pepper, chopped
8	ounces Crab Meat mixed with 1 teaspoon Creole seasoning
3	tablespoons clarified butter

In a medium sauce pan over medium heat, add clarified butter until heated. Sauté onions, garlic, and bell pepper for about 2 minutes making sure to retain shape and texture; mix in pecans and Creole seasoning, blend well. Add crab meat and toss together. Keep warm or reheat in oven.

OK, LETS ASSEMBLE!

Dredge the Drum fillets in a large shallow platter containing the pecan crust mixture, pressing the mixture to the fish. Once breaded, cook the fish in a large frying pan containing the clarified butter at medium heat about 3 minutes each side.

Remove Drum Fish to a pre-warmed serving platter or directly to warmed dinner plates.

Divide Pecan Crab Chutney into 4 servings. Place one serving atop each pre-cooked Drum fillet. Drizzle with warm Lemon sauce and viola! Enjoy!!

ELIZABETH ON 37TH STREET

105 East 37th Street
Savannah, Georgia 31401
(912) 236-5547
Reservations required • Open daily 6 - 10 pm
Amex, Visa, MC, DC, & Discover accepted
www.elizabthon37th.com

This elegant turn-of-the-century Southern mansion is the setting for Chef Elizabeth Terry's stunning new regional cooking based on traditional recipes. The seasonal menu makes use of the bounty of fresh local seafood and produce, highlighted with herbs from our own gardens. The personable and efficient staff is pleased to continue the time-honored tradition of Southern hospitality, serving fine food, spirits, and perfectly matched wine from the carefully chosen wine list.

FROM KAREN BUTCH AT ELIZABETH ON 37TH:

Jim Williams and friends regularly dined at his favorite table at Elizabeth on 37th. But I recall the frequent phone calls just before the evening's end: "Can I still come in?", "Of course". He arrived alone and his cocktail was waiting. He loved working folks so he treated the staff like buddies, and he loved to tell me stories and gossip, often trying to raise an eyebrow or make me squeal with laughter. He enjoyed good food and always finished with the pecan almond tart and, took one home to his mother. I can't promise that she received it.

BLACK-EYED PEA SOUP

1	16 ounce package dried black-eyed peas	1	cup dry sherry
8	cups chicken broth	1	cup wild rice, cooked
3	ham hocks	½	cup fresh red peppers (or ¼ cup dried)
2	cups onion, minced	1	cup smoked chicken or
1	cup celery, minced		sausage, drained and
3	cloves garlic, minced		diced
	Black pepper to taste		

In a large Dutch oven, cover peas with water and let soak overnight. Drain if needed. Add broth and ham hocks and cook, covered, for 1 hour, skimming when necessary. Add onions, celery, and garlic and simmer 30 minutes longer. Remove ham hocks, cut meat from the bones, and return meat to soup with sherry, rice, red pepper, and smoked meat; season lightly with black pepper.

Serves 8 to 10.

OYSTER AND SAUSAGE TURNOVER

1	pound spicy bulk sausage	¼	cup cream cheese
1	pint fresh oysters	¼	cup Asiago cheese,
½	cup raw milk Cheddar cheese or mild Cheddar, grated		grated
		1	8 inch pie crust (favorite recipe)

Sauté sausage and drain on a paper towel. Place oysters under the broiler for 1 minute to firm. Combine sausage, oysters, and cheeses and drain mixture in a sieve. Prepare piecrust dough. Divide dough into quarters and roll out each quarter into a circle. Place 2 or more rounded spoonfuls of sausage mixture on half of each circle; then fold other half over mixture to form a half-moon shape, sealing edges with a fork. Continue until sausage mixture is used up. Bake at 400 degrees for 10 minutes. Serves 4.

POTATO CRUSTED RED SNAPPER

5	Idaho potatoes, peeled minced and grated	1	tablespoon finely lemon zest
1	tablespoon salt	½	cup butter, melted
1	cup freshly grated Asiago ground cheese (Parmesan may be substituted)	¾	tablespoon freshly black pepper
		6	6 ounce red snapper fillets

Preheat oven to 425 degrees. Bring a large pot of lightly salted water to boil; add grated potatoes and boil for 30 seconds, then drain. Plunge into ice bath and drain immediately. Spread potatoes on a plate or baking sheet to dry. Toss with melted butter, salt, pepper, cheese, and lemon zest. Lightly coat each fish fillet with potato, pressing potato with fingertips.

Place the potato crusted fish on a lightly oiled baking sheet and roast fish for 15 to 20 minutes in the oven until lightly browned and cooked through. Yields 6 servings. Serve with Brussels Sprouts Hash (see below).

BRUSSELS SPROUTS HASH:

3	cups quartered Brussels sprouts, core removed	¼	cup cooked and chopped bacon
½	cup ¼ -inch diced Vidalia onions	1	cup heavy cream
2	cups chopped crookneck squash, cut in half, soft seed center, discarded and outer part cut into ½ -inch dice	½	cup rich chicken stock, degreased Fresh-cracked black pepper to taste

Place all ingredients in large sauté pan and cover. Cook over high heat and bring just to a boil. Remove lid and continue to cook over high heat until all liquid is completely reduced and vegetables are tender, approximately 7 to 10 minutes. Stir and season to taste with cracked pepper. Serves 4 to 6.

PECAN ALMOND TART

¾	cup light Karo syrup
½	cup sugar
3	tablespoons unsalted butter, chilled
3	eggs
1	teaspoon vanilla
1	cup pecans, chopped and toasted
⅓	cup sliced almonds

Preheat oven to 375 degrees.

1 batch of your favorite pie crust for a 1-crust pie - fit into a 9 inch pie pan.

In a medium sauce pan over medium heat, stir the syrup and the sugar together and bring to a boil. Continue cooking for about 2 minutes until the sugar is dissolved. Remove from the heat and stir in the cold butter. Cool the syrup for 5 minutes. Whip the eggs in a bowl with a whisk to break the yolks, then whisk in the syrup and vanilla. Pour into the shell. Sprinkle with pecans, then finally with the almonds and bake for 30 minutes.

Cool before serving. Serve with a scoop of vanilla ice cream. Serves 10.

Trivia: In Chapter 17 "A Hole in the Floor," Prentiss Crowe announced that Jim Williams' meals would be catered by three different restaurants and delivered to him in the cold confines of the Chatham County Jail. Can you name the three restaurants? (We highly recommend them, of course).

LIGHT CHESS PIE
WITH CHOCOLATE AND RASPBERRIES

3	extra large eggs	1	teaspoon rum
1	cup sugar	¼	cup semisweet chocolate
⅓	cup sour cream		chips
¼	cup cake flour	½	pint fresh raspberries
1	8 inch pie crust, baked	½	pint heavy whipping
1	tablespoon butter		cream
1	tablespoon Grand Marnier or crème de cassis		

Separate eggs and beat whites until stiff but not dry. In another bowl, beat yolks about 4 minutes until pale yellow. Add sugar and mix well, then add sour cream and cake flour until well blended. Gently fold in egg whites. Fill pie shell with mixture and bake at 325 degrees for 10 minutes until custard is set and light brown. Cool. In a small saucepan, make a glaze by melting butter and rum until blended. Remove from heat. Add chocolate. *Do not cook* the chocolate; the hot butter-rum mixture will melt it. Stir and cool. Spread a thin layer of chocolate on the cooled pie. Cover pie with raspberries. Whip cream with Grand Marnier or crème de cassis and pipe or spoon over top of pie in desired design.

Yields 1 pie.

Johnny Harris Restaurant

1651 East Victory Drive
Savannah, Georgia 31404
(912) 354-7810
www.johnnyharris.com

In the spring of 1924, a star was born in the sleepy southern town of Savannah, Georgia. Not the type of star you might find at a Hollywood gala, but the type that burns bright in the eyes of the generations that would grow up dancing and dining at Johnny Harris Restaurant. Initially erected at the corner of Bee Road and Victory Drive, the restaurant was hardly more than a roadside Bar-B-Que shack. Built with a white clapboard exterior dotted with black shutters and a sawdust floor inside, Johnny Harris Restaurant would rise from its humble beginnings to enjoy the loyal following and reputation of today, as one of the largest and most popular full service restaurants in the city. In 1936 the restaurant's present location was completed. Some say it was the first air-conditioned dining room in the South. Over the years hundreds of thousands of people from all walks of life have passed through the restaurant. When Jackie Gleason's train rumbled through Savannah it would stop long enough to send out for Johnny Harris' succulent spareribs.

Renowned songwriter Johnny Mercer, a Savannah native, always ate fried chicken in the restaurant's kitchen when he was in town. The list of notable patrons goes on and on, from Robert Mitchem to Bob Hope to John Berendt, who wrote *Midnight in the Garden of Good and Evil*. While incarcerated Jim Williams would get supper from Johnny Harris's one night and Elizabeth on 37th the next.

Through the years the recipes have been handed down so as to keep that same special blend and flavor that it started with so many years ago.

Note: Johnny Harris has always had a special place in my heart. I have taken great pride in knowing that my grandfather, Jacob Sullivan, was one of the master carpenters to help build this magnificent restaurant.

PASTA PUTTANESCA SAUCE

Phil Donaldson, owner, writes: "This Italian sauce is probably the best-tasting spaghetti sauce we have ever tested. However, it is not very well known. The name means 'prostitute's sauce,' and the story goes that the ladies would prepare the sauce and put it on their windowsills, and the smell was so fabulous that it attracted clients for them."

¼	cup olive oil	¼	cup drained capers
4	cloves garlic, crushed	8	anchovy fillets, minced
2	14 ounce cans Italian plum tomatoes, coarsely chopped, juice reserved	¼	cup chopped fresh Italian parsley or basil
½	cup sliced black olives	1 ½	teaspoons dried oregano
¼	cup dry red wine	½	teaspoon dried rosemary
		⅛	teaspoon red pepper flakes

Heat the olive oil in a heavy skillet over medium heat; sauté the garlic until translucent. Add the tomatoes, and their reserved juice, then stir in the olives, wine, capers, anchovies, parsley, dried herbs, and pepper flakes.

Bring to a boil, cover, and reduce to a slow simmer. Simmer for 45 minutes. Serve over pasta, (like a spaghetti sauce).
Serves 4 to 6.

BAKED FLOUNDER

1 ½ pounds flounder fillets*
     Salt and pepper
3   ounces sherry

1 ½ cups (2 sticks) melted
     butter
2   cups bread crumbs

Preheat oven to 375 degrees. Lay flounder fillets in a buttered 13x9x2-inch baking dish and season with salt and pepper to taste.

Pour sherry over the fish; then pour on half of the butter. Cover the fish with bread crumbs and pour the remaining butter over the crumbs. Bake for 15 minutes.

Serves 3 to 4.

* Cooked lobster meat or raw scallops may be substituted for flounder.

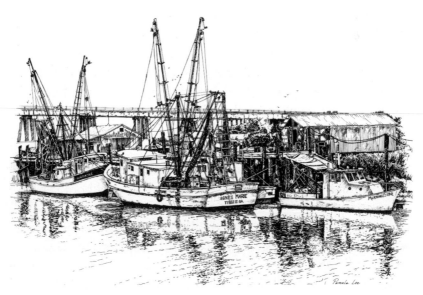

Pamela Lee

THE LADY & SONS

102 W Congress St
Savannah, Georgia 31401
(912)233-2600
(912)233-8283 fax (912)232-4332 catering fax
www.ladyandsons.com

Hours Monday - Saturday
Lunch: 11 am - 3pm
Dinner: Begins at 5pm

Sunday
Lunch buffet only 11am - 5pm

Paula Deen grew up in Albany, Georgia spending hours at a time in her Grandmother Paul's kitchen. Grandmother Paul was a wonderful cook, and she handed down her love of cooking to her three daughters. They in turn passed this love on to Paula.

In 1989, newly divorced and unemployed, and living in Savannah, Georgia, Paula was determined to succeed. She invested her last two hundred dollars in a catering business that she started with her two sons, Jamie and Bobby. After a few years of local catering, high demand helped her small-scale business evolve into The Lady and Sons Restaurant where she and her sons function as owners, proprietors, chefs, and hosts.

All their hard work has paid off. In their new restaurant Paula offers cooking classes; she is always writing a cookbook; she has a cooking show on The Food Network; and now she is playing a role in an upcoming movie. With all this it is hard to believe she has time for herself, but she has recently re-married and seemingly enjoys her lifestyle.

Paula is a real asset to the community and a good friend as well. I know that The Lady and Sons will be on your scheduled stop. God Bless You and all you do. Deborah & Shane

CHEESE BISCUITS

2	cups all-purpose flour	½	cup Crisco shortening
1	tablespoon baking powder	¾	cup grated Cheddar
1	teaspoon sugar		cheese
1	cup buttermilk		

Preheat oven to 350 degrees. Mix flour, baking powder, and sugar together using a fork; cut in shortening until it resembles cornmeal. Add cheese. Stir in buttermilk all at one time just until blended. Do not over stir. Drop by tablespoonfuls (you could use an ice cream scoop to give biscuit's a nicer shape) onto a well-greased baking sheet. Bake for 12 to 15 minutes.
Yields 8 large biscuits.

HOECAKES

These hoecakes have become a favorite with The Lady & Sons Guests. Use them to soak up that good pot liquor from turnip or collard greens. After the plate is completely sopped clean, save one to eat as a dessert along with maple syrup.

1	cup self-rising flour	¼	cup buttermilk
1	cup self-rising cornmeal	⅓	cup plus 1 tablespoon
2	eggs		water
1	tablespoon sugar	¼	cup vegetable oil or
	Oil or butter for frying		bacon grease

Mix all ingredients well except for frying oil. Heat oil in a skillet over medium heat; drop mixture by tablespoonfuls into hot skillet. Use approximately 2 tablespoons batter per hoecake. Brown until crisp; turn and brown on other side. Drain on paper towels. Leftover batter will keep in refrigerator for up to 2 days.
   Yields approximately 17 Cakes.

CHICKEN GEORGIA

4	tablespoons (½ stick) butter	2	tablespoons minced shallots
4	skinless, boneless chicken breast halves	¼	teaspoon salt
1	cup sliced fresh mushrooms	¼	teaspoon pepper
		4	ounces grated mozzarella cheese

Melt butter over medium heat. Add mushrooms and shallots and sprinkle with salt and pepper. Cook 10 minutes. Add chicken and cook 10 minutes on each side, or until tender. Transfer chicken to platter and sprinkle with grated cheese. Top with mushroom mixture. Cover and let stand 5 minutes or until cheese has melted.

Serves 4 to 6.

Fun Fact: The official release of "*Midnight in the Garden of Good and Evil*" was January 1994. The first printing was 25,000 copies. The price was $23. A true First Edition has several distinctions; one being on page 11, seven lines from the bottom is the typo "fmr Madeira" instead of for Madeira.

CHICKEN DIVAN OR CHICKEN FLORENTINE

According to Paula, of the many chicken casserole–type dishes she has eaten, this one is just about the best. Adding broccoli makes it divan; adding spinach makes it Florentine. "Everyone asks for this recipe."

2	10 ounce packages frozen chopped broccoli (if making divan)	1	cup grated sharp Cheddar cheese
2	10 ounce packages frozen chopped spinach (if making Florentine)	1	tablespoon fresh lemon juice
6	chicken breast halves (about 4 pounds), cooked, boned, and shredded	1	teaspoon curry powder
			Salt and pepper
		½	cup dry white wine
		½	cup freshly grated Parmesan cheese
2	10 ¾ ounce cans condensed cream of mushroom soup	½	cup soft bread crumbs
		2	tablespoons butter
1	cup mayonnaise	1	cup sour cream

Remove the outer wrappers from the boxes of broccoli or spinach. Open one end of each box; microwave on full power for 2 minutes, until thawed. Drain the broccoli or spinach and put into a large bowl. Add the shredded chicken.

In a medium bowl, combine the soup, mayonnaise, sour cream, Cheddar cheese, lemon juice, curry powder, salt and pepper to taste, and wine; whisk together to make a sauce. Pour the sauce over the broccoli or spinach and chicken. Mix well with a spatula.

Place the mixture into an 11x7-inch casserole dish or two 9-inch square disposable aluminum foil pans the have been sprayed with vegetable oil cooking spray. Pat down evenly and smooth with a spatula. Combine the Parmesan cheese and bread crumbs and sprinkle over the top; dot with the butter.

Wrap the uncooked casserole(s) securely with plastic wrap, then with aluminum foil. Place each pan into a plastic freezer bag and seal. Freeze. Prepare a label with these instructions: Allow casserole to thaw 24 hours in the refrigerator. When ready to bake, remove the plastic wrap and foil. Bake, uncovered, at 350 degrees for about 40 minutes, until bubbly.

If serving immediately, bake, uncovered, in a 350 degree oven for about 30 minutes, until bubbly. Serves 6 to 8.

CHICKEN POT PIE

1	10 ¼ ounce can condensed Cheddar cheese soup	3	carrots, sliced, cooked and drained
1	10 ¼ ounce can condensed cream of celery soup		Salt and pepper to taste
½	cup milk	1	pastry for top and bottom (see pastry recipe)
1	chicken, skinned, cooked, boned and cubed		Butter to dot pastry
1	10 ounce package frozen green peas or 1 8 ounce can, drained	1	medium onion, diced

In a large saucepan, heat soups and milk; stir in chicken, onion, peas, carrots, and salt and pepper. Cook until mixture boils. Remove from heat. Preheat oven to 350 degrees. Pour into pastry-lined 13x9x2-inch pan. Cut pastry for top into strips. Lay over pie filling in a lattice style; dot with butter. Bake for 45 minutes until golden brown.

Serves 6 to 8.

PASTRY

3	cups all-purpose flour	¾	cup Crisco shortening
1	teaspoon salt		Ice water
¼	teaspoon baking powder		

Sift together flour, salt, and baking powder. Cut in shortening with pastry blender until pieces are the size of small peas. Sprinkle 1 to 2 tablespoons of ice water over part of mixture. Gently toss with fork; push to side of bowl. Repeat until all is moistened. Form into 2 balls. Flatten each on a lightly floured surface by pressing with edge of hand three times across in both directions. With a floured rolling pin, roll out on floured surface. Roll from center to edge until ⅛ inch thick.

BEAUFORT SHRIMP PIE

In the Carolina Sea Islands, a "pie" does not necessarily have a crust. This shrimp casserole is a superb luncheon dish and is one of these pies.

½	cup chopped onion	2	cups milk
¼	cup chopped green bell pepper	2	eggs
			Salt and pepper
2	tablespoons butter	3	strips bacon
3	cups cooked and peeled shrimp	2	cups soft bread crumbs

Sauté the onion and bell pepper in butter until soft. In a casserole dish, make layers of the shrimp, bread crumbs, onions and peppers. Beat together the milk, eggs, and salt and pepper to taste, and pour over the shrimp. Cut each strip of bacon into 4 pieces. Lay bacon on top of the casserole and bake at 325 degrees until the filling is set and the bacon is brown. Serves 6-8.

FRIED GRITS CAKES WITH SAUSAGE

1	pound hot bulk sausage	2	tablespoons grated orange zest
4	cups chicken broth		Vegetable oil
1	cup stone-ground yellow grits		

In a large skillet over medium heat, combine the sausage and orange zest, stirring to break up the sausage. Sauté until browned and then drain; set aside. In a large saucepan over medium heat, bring the chicken broth to a boil. Slowly stir in the grits. Reduce the heat, cover, and simmer for 20 minutes, stirring occasionally. Stir the sausage into the grits. Spread the mixture in 13x9-inch baking pan to cool, then refrigerate until well chilled. Cut the chilled grits into squares and sauté in vegetable oil until crisp and browned on both sides. Serves 6.

SAVANNAH BOW TIES

These are some of Paula's favorites

1	sheet frozen puff pastry from a 17 ¼ ounce package	2	teaspoons milk
½	cup almond paste		Flour for dusting the work surface
1	egg, separated		Granulated or coarse
¼	cup packed light brown sugar		sugar, for sprinkling

CHOCOLATE DIPPING SAUCE:

¾	cup granulated sugar	2	cups whipping cream
2	tablespoons cornstarch	1	egg yolk, beaten
¼	teaspoon salt	½	teaspoon vanilla extract
6	1 ½ ounce milk chocolate bars		

Let the puff pastry stand at room temperature for 20 minutes, or until easy to roll. Preheat the oven to 400 degrees. Line cookie sheets with aluminum foil, parchment paper, or nonstick baking mats.

Crumble the almond paste into a small mixing bowl. Add the egg yolk, brown sugar, and milk. Beat with an electric mixer at medium speed until well combined. The filling will be very stiff.

Unfold the pastry on lightly floured surface. Roll out into a 14-inch square. Cut the square in half with a fluted pastry wheel.

Drop dollops of filling uniformly over one of the rectangles of dough. Spray a piece of wax paper with vegetable oil cooking spray and use it to press the filling evenly over the dough. Spray the wax paper as often as necessary to prevent filling from sticking.

Place the remaining rectangle on top of the filling. Using a fluted pastry wheel, cut the dough crosswise into fourteen 1-inch-wide strips, then cut each strip in half to make 28 pieces. Twist each piece twice. Place the twists about 2 inches apart on the prepared cookie sheets. Brush the twists with lightly beaten egg white. Sprinkle with granulated sugar.

Bake for 12 to 15 minutes, until golden brown. Transfer to wire racks to cool.

While the cookies are cooling, make the Chocolate Dipping Sauce: in a saucepan, stir together the sugar, cornstarch, and salt. Crumble the chocolate bars in one at a time. Gradually stir in the cream. Cook stirring over low heat until the chocolate is melted. In a small bowl, combine ½ cup of the hot chocolate sauce with the egg yolk. Add the yolk mixture to the pot and cook, stirring, until the sauce comes to a boil. Remove from the heat. Stir in vanilla and pour into a serving bowl. Any remaining sauce can be poured into custard cups, refrigerated, and served as pudding.

Serve the cookies with Chocolate Dipping Sauce.

Makes 28 cookies.

IS IT REALLY BETTER THAN SEX? CAKE

1	18 ¼ ounce box yellow cake mix (plus ingredients to prepare)	1	3.4 ounce box French vanilla pudding (plus ingredients to prepare
1	20 ounce can crushed pineapple	1 ½	cups heavy cream
1 ⅓	cups sugar	1	cup flaked, sweetened coconut, toasted*

Preheat oven to 350 degrees. Grease a 13x9x2-inch pan.

Prepare cake as directed on package. Pour into prepared pan. Bake 30 to 35 minutes. While cake is baking, combine pineapple and 1 cup of the sugar in a saucepan; bring to a boil over medium heat, stirring constantly. Remove from heat and allow to cool slightly. Remove cake from oven and pierce holes in cake with a fork. Pour pineapple mixture over hot cake. Prepare pudding according to package directions. Spread over cake and refrigerate until thoroughly chilled. Before serving, beat cream and remaining sugar together with an electric mixer until stiff. Cover top of cake with whipped cream and sprinkle with toasted coconut.

* To toast coconut, spread in a thin layer on a cookie sheet. Place in a 350 degree oven. Watch very carefully because it can burn quickly. Stir as often as needed to ensure it browns evenly.

SOUTHWEST GEORGIA POUND CAKE

1　cup (2 sticks) butter, softened
3　cups sugar
6　eggs
3　cups all-purpose flour
½　teaspoon baking powder

½　teaspoon salt
1　cup heavy cream
2　teaspoons pure vanilla extract (you may use lemon or almond flavoring instead)

Generously grease and flour a 10-inch bundt pan.

Using an electric mixer, cream butter and sugar together until fluffy. Add eggs one at a time, beating well after each addition. Sift together flour, baking powder, and salt. Alternately add flour mixture and heavy cream to butter-sugar mixture, beginning and ending with flour. Stir in flavoring. Pour batter into prepared pan. Place in a cold oven, set oven temperature at 325 degrees, and bake for 1 ¼ hours without opening oven door. Bake for an additional 15 minutes if necessary. Remove from oven and cool in pan for 15 minutes. Invert cake onto cake plate, and for a real treat, serve yourself a slice while it is still warm.

Trivia: Who willed herself to die two days from her birthday because she felt that the high points in her life had come and gone with the 1930's and 1940's? (#90)

DOUBLE RUM CAKE

1   18 ½ ounce package yellow cake mix
1   3 ½ ounce package instant vanilla pudding mix
½   cup rum, light or dark
½   cup vegetable oil
4   large eggs
½   cup chopped pecans

RUM SYRUP:
1   cup sugar
½   cup (1 stick) margarine
¼   cup rum, light or dark

Preheat the oven to 325 degrees. Liberally spray a non-stick 2-quart bundt pan with vegetable oil cooking spray.

Using an electric mixer at low speed, blend the cake mix, pudding mix, rum, oil, and ½ cup water. Add the eggs, one at a time, beating well after each addition.

Evenly distribute the pecans in the bottom of the prepared bundt pan. Pour the batter on top of the pecans. Bake for 50 to 55 minutes, until a knife inserted an inch from the center comes out clean; do not remove the cake from the pan.

Make the rum syrup: In a small saucepan, bring the sugar, margarine, rum, and ¼ cup water to a boil and cook for 3 minutes. With a fork, make holes in the top of the cake. Pour the syrup over the cake and let sit for 30 minutes while the syrup is absorbed.

Invert the pan onto a serving plate. Allow it to sit for several minutes; the cake will loosen from the pan.

Serves 12 to 16.

THE OLDE PINK HOUSE
RESTAURANT AND TAVERN

23 Abercorn Street
Savannah, Georgia 31401
(912) 232-4286
Dinner
5:30 P.M. until 10:30 P.M. Daily
Reservations
(Preferred)

The Olde Pink House was built in the Georgian style by James Habersham, Jr. in 1771. Savannah's oldest mansion has taken on a pink tinge from its red bricks, through time, the color has seeped through the white stucco.

As with most old mansions in Savannah, spirits are still believed to roam about. Though the ghost of James Habersham has never been seen in The Olde Pink House, everyone knows who lights the candles, rearranges the furniture and twirls the chandelier —all are familiar occurrences.

Today, we enjoy The Olde Pink House tavern; listening to Gail Thurmond playing jazz on the piano and singing Johnny Mercer songs along with her well-written Southern ballads. Add a mint Julep, or two, and one of their delicious meals; it's a great way to end a wonderful day in our charming city. Who knows, the spirits may be roaming about that evening.

THE OLDE PINK HOUSE'S
SHE-CRAB SOUP

1 ½	cups onion, chopped	3	ounces crab roe
1 ½	cups celery, chopped	¾	cup plain flour
½	cup red bell pepper, chopped	3	quarts milk
1	tablespoon fresh thyme, chopped	1	pound blue or white crabmeat
1	cup butter		Salt and pepper to taste

In a large, heavy saucepan; sauté onion, celery, pepper, and thyme in butter. Add crab roe. Stir in flour. Add milk, stirring with a wire whisk. Bring mixture to 200 degrees, stirring often. Add crabmeat. Season with salt and pepper and serve. Serves 6 to 8.

THE OLDE PINK HOUSE'S
RIVERFRONT GUMBO

1	pound meaty ham bone	1	teaspoon salt
1	chicken or turkey carcass with some meat intact	¼	teaspoon freshly ground black pepper
1	pound beef marrow bones	1	cup beef stock
1	16 ounce can tomatoes, chopped	1	tablespoon butter
		2 ½	cups sliced okra
3	stalks celery, chopped	1	17 ounce can whole-kernel corn
2	medium onions, chopped		
1	large green pepper, chopped	½	cup red wine
1	teaspoon or more cumin		Chopped parsley

Place ham bone, chicken carcass, and beef marrow in a large, heavy sauce pan. Add tomatoes, celery, onions, green pepper, and seasonings. Cover with water and bring to a boil; reduce heat, cover, and simmer for 2 hours, stirring occasionally to prevent sticking. Remove the bones, leaving the meat. Add beef stock. Stir in butter, okra, corn, and red wine. Simmer 30 to 40 minutes. Taste and adjust seasonings. Garnish with parsley before serving. Serves 8.

ALMOND CRUSTED TILAPIA WITH FRESH LOCAL SHRIMP AND HERB BUTTER SAUCE

4-6	ounces Tilapia filets
12	large shrimp (peeled and deveined)
2	ounces heavy cream
2	ounces salted butter
2	ounces white wine
1	tablespoon blended fresh parsley, chives, basil, and thyme (Almond bread crumb coating)

ALMOND BREAD CRUMB COATING:

1	cup sliced almonds
⅓	cup bread crumbs
¼	cup flour

Dip the Tilapia filets in milk and lightly season with salt and pepper. Coat filets with almond bread crumb coating. In a large skillet with melted butter, cook the filets on medium to medium low heat on both sides until done (approximately 4 minutes). Take filets out of the skillet and add the shrimp to the skillet; lightly season with salt and pepper. Add herbs, wine, cream and butter. Cook until shrimp are done (approximately 2 minutes). Pour sauce on top of the filets at once and place shrimp on each filet.

Trivia: What 1950's novel is a reflection of Savannah's "Glorious" isolation? (#88)

PECAN-CRUSTED CHICKEN

4	5 to 6 ounce boneless chicken breasts
	Salt and pepper to taste
½	cup milk or half and half
1	egg
1	cup ground pecans
¼	cup bread crumbs
½	cup flour
4	tablespoons vegetable oil
1	cup blackberry preserves
1	cup red wine

Rinse the chicken and pat dry. Sprinkle with salt and pepper. Combine the milk and egg in a bowl and mix well. Combine the pecans, bread crumbs and flour in a shallow dish and mix well. Dip the chicken in the milk mixture; coat with the pecan mixture. Sauté the chicken in the oil in a skillet until brown on all sides, turning occasionally; transfer the chicken to a baking pan. Bake at 350 degrees for 8 to 10 minutes or until cooked through. Heat the preserves and wine in a saucepan, stirring occasionally. Serve with the chicken.

Yield: 4 servings.

Trivia: Name at least three of Johnny Mercer's songs. (#87)

THE OLDE PINK HOUSE'S SHERRY TRIFLE

1 ½	quarts milk	½	cup sherry
1 ½	cups sugar	2	cups cream
2	tablespoons cornstarch	1 ½	pounds of pound cake,
6	eggs		sliced
	Raspberry or		
	strawberry preserves		

Pour milk into the top of a double boiler over hot (not boiling) water. In a mixing bowl, beat together sugar, cornstarch, and eggs until smooth. Add to milk and heat slowly, stirring constantly, until the mixture thickens. Set aside to cool. Add sherry to the cooled custard. In another bowl, whip the cream and set aside. Arrange cake slices in a 13x9¼x2-inch baking pan. Spread with preserves; then top with a layer of custard and a layer of whip cream. Repeat until all ingredients are used. Chill.

Serves 6 to 8.

Fun Facts: "Midnight" is currently in its 107th Hardcover printing with sales exceeding 2,500,000 copies. Foreign rights to "The Book" have been sold in twenty seven countries.

THE PIRATES' HOUSE RESTAURANT

45 South At The Pirates' House
20 East Broad Street
Savannah, Georgia 31401
(912) 233-1881
www.thepirateshouse.com

Savannah's famous Pirates' House is located on one of the most historic spots in Georgia. It is here that Trustees Garden, the first experimental garden in America, was located. When General Oglethorpe and his little band of colonists arrived from England in 1733, they came ashore in the vicinity of the present City Hall on Bull and Bay Streets, approximately seven blocks due west of The Pirates' House. There they pitched their tents to found the City of Savannah.

Since 1753, The Pirates' House has been welcoming visitors to Savannah with a bounty of delicious food and drink and rousing good times. Situated a scant block from the Savannah River, The Pirates' House first opened as an inn for seafarers, and fast became a rendezvous for blood-thirsty pirates and sailors from the Seven Seas. Here seamen drank their grog and discoursed, sailor fashion, on their exotic high seas adventures from Singapore to Bombay and from London to Port Said.

The entire family will enjoy Savannah's most intriguing restaurant. At The Pirates' House, our most precious treasure is our food, acclaimed for over three decades. Our extensive menu includes dishes for all tastes and our varied selection of scandalous desserts is sure to delight. Like a tale of the high seas, The Pirates' House rambles in all directions.

While visiting Savannah I hope that time will permit you to visit The Pirates' House and experience one of their 15 unique dining rooms.

Eggs Benedict

8 English muffin halves, toasted

8 thin slices boiled ham, lightly sautéed in butter

8 poached eggs, just cooked or reheated (see below)

Salt and pepper

1 recipe Blender Hollandaise sauce, see recipe

Finely chopped fresh parsley for garnish, optional

Poached Eggs

Fill a large, deep skillet with 1 ½ inches of water. Add 1 tablespoon white vinegar and bring just to a simmer. Crack egg on edge of skillet; holding shell just above water, lower egg very gently into water. Set timer for 4 minutes. Immediately repeat with remaining eggs. When timer goes off, remove eggs carefully with slotted spoon in the order in which they were added to pan. Use immediately, or drop into a bowl of cold water. Poached eggs may be stored in their bowl of water, uncovered, in the refrigerator for 2 or 3 days. To reheat, drop into a pan of barely simmering salted water and leave for 2 minutes, then remove with a slotted spoon and pat dry with a towel. Any unattractive extra egg white may be trimmed with scissors or a knife.

To Assemble:

Toast muffins and place on serving plates. Make Hollandaise Sauce; keep warm. Sauté ham and place a slice of ham on each muffin. Poach eggs (or reheat previously poached ones); place one on each muffin. Salt and pepper eggs and cover with Hollandaise Sauce. Sprinkle with parsley if desired, and serve immediately. Serves 4, allowing 2 eggs apiece (see recipe on page 41).

BLENDER HOLLANDAISE SAUCE

3	egg yolks	½	cup butter
	Pinch cayenne pepper		(no substitute)
1	tablespoon lemon juice		

Put egg yolks, cayenne, and lemon juice in blender and blend on high for 5 seconds. Heat butter in a small saucepan until boiling. With blender on high speed, pour butter slowly through small opening in top. Run for 30 seconds. Taste and add more lemon juice or cayenne if necessary. If sauce is too thick, blend in boiling water 1 teaspoon at a time. Serve immediately. Do not save leftover sauce.

Note: This recipe will not work in a food processor.

Pamela Lee

OYSTERS SAVANNAH

TOPPING

1	bell pepper	1	teaspoon freshly ground
2	ribs celery		black pepper
½	pound raw bacon	1	teaspoon salt
1	2 ounce jar pimientos	¾	teaspoon Tabasco sauce

Chop everything fine in a food processor. Process until topping is well-blended and holds together.

2	dozen shell oysters or	Rock salt
1	pint oysters, drained	

Preheat oven to broil. Lay oysters on the half shell on a bed of rock salt on a metal baking sheet with sides. Cover each oyster with 1 tablespoon topping. Or place several oysters in individual scallop shells or metal crab shells. Spread a layer of topping over oysters and place on rock salt. Broil 4 to 5 inches from heat until topping is browned and bubbling, 10 to 12 minutes. Drain off any grease. Serve immediately.

Note: Besides natural oyster shells, metal crab shells work best. The topping sits above the edge of the shell and as it cooks, the accumulated fat runs off into the rock salt. If the sides of the baking dish are too high, the grease pools on top of the oysters and the topping will not crisp.

Trivia: Danny Hansford believed he would receive what specifically if he were to die in Mercer House? Did he indeed receive it? (#11)

SAVANNAH RED RICE

4	slices bacon	1	8 ounce can tomato sauce
1	medium onion, chopped	1	teaspoon sugar
2	ribs celery, chopped	1	teaspoon salt
1	small bell pepper, chopped		Black pepper to taste
			Tabasco sauce to taste,
2	cups raw rice, rinsed well		(should be spicy)
1	1 pound can tomatoes, drained and chopped (reserve juice)		

Fry bacon in a heavy pot until crisp; remove. Sauté onions, celery, and bell pepper in bacon grease until onions are translucent. Crumble bacon; return to pot. Add rice; stir to coat with grease. Add tomatoes. Measure reserved tomato juice and tomato sauce; add water to make 2 ½ cups (total) liquid. Pour over rice and bring to a boil, stirring occasionally. Immediately lower heat until barely simmering, cover pot and set timer for 20 minutes. After 20 minutes, remove from heat and let sit at least 20 minutes. Do not peek. After 20 minutes, fluff with a fork and serve.

ORANGE-CREAM CHEESE-
PECAN DRESSING

1	8 ounce package cream cheese, softened	2	tablespoons milk
1	6 ounce can concentrated orange juice, thawed (not diluted)	1 ½	teaspoons sugar
		¼	teaspoon salt
		¼	cup chopped pecans

Beat cream cheese until smooth. Add orange juice, milk, sugar and salt; beat until smooth. Stir in pecans. Refrigerate 8 hours or overnight to blend flavors. Remove from refrigerator an hour before serving to soften. Use on fruit salads.

SAVANNAH SALAD

DRESSING

¼	cup olive oil	1	teaspoon salt
¼	cup vegetable oil	½	teaspoon black pepper
¼	cup red wine vinegar	1	teaspoon dried oregano
1	large clove garlic, finely chopped	1	teaspoon freshly grated Parmesan cheese
1	small sweet onion, sliced thin	1	tablespoon water

Place above ingredients in a jar with tight-fitting lid and shake to combine—best made early in day.

4	hard-boiled eggs		Croutons, see below
1	head each Bibb, Boston and Leaf lettuce (3 heads total)	½	cup chopped toasted pecans

Sieve egg yolks; chop egg whites very fine. Wash lettuce and dry well. Reserve Bibb lettuce leaves to line 8 cold salad plates. Tear remaining lettuce into bite-sized pieces. Toss with dressing (you may not need it all) being sure to use onions. Divide lettuce evenly among plates. Sprinkle egg yolks and whites, pecans and croutons over salads in an artistic manner. Serves 8.

Note: To make croutons, trim crust from 4 slices of firm white bread. Cut into tiny cubes. Heat 2 tablespoons of olive oil, 3 teaspoons butter, and 1 clove finely chopped garlic in a skillet. Sauté bread cubes until golden brown. Drain on paper towels and store lightly covered until ready to use.

OKRA GUMBO SOUP

2	1 pound can tomatoes, coarsely chopped	3	ounces ham, diced
1	tablespoon tomato paste	5	cups water
1	medium onion, coarsely chopped	1	teaspoon salt
1	small bell pepper, coarsely chopped	½	teaspoon pepper
2	ribs celery, coarsely chopped	¾	teaspoon Angostura bitters, optional
		1	pound frozen sliced okra

Combine all ingredients except okra in a soup pot. Bring to a boil, lower heat, and simmer 1 hour. Add okra and simmer for 20 minutes more. Serves 6 to 8.

Note: Angostura bitters add a certain something, but don't go out and a buy a bottle just for this recipe.

SEAFOOD GUMBO

1	recipe Okra Gumbo Soup, (see above)	1	pound crabmeat, picked over for shells
1 ½	cups cooked and peeled baby shrimp (frozen are fine, but thaw and rinse them)		

Five minutes before serving, add seafood and heat through. Serves 6 to 8.

Fun Fact: In October 1992, John Berendt sent the finished manuscript of "Midnight" to his New York literary agent. She rejected it, too local, she said. John found a new agent and the hardcover edition stayed on the New York Times bestseller list for a record breaking 216 weeks.

RING TUM DITTY

12	ounces bacon, chopped		Dried basil
2	cups chopped onions		Salt and pepper
2	16 ounce cans whole tomatoes, juice reserved	3	cups (¾ pound) grated extra-sharp Cheddar cheese
1	16 ounce can whole-kernel corn	4-6	baking potatoes, baked

Sauté the bacon and onions in a heavy pot until the bacon is crisp and the onion is translucent. Drain off the fat. Drain the tomato juice into the pot; squish the tomatoes through your fingers into the pot. Add the corn, and basil, salt, and pepper to taste, and simmer the mixture for 10 to 15 minutes or until desired thickness. Add the cheese and stir until melted. Spoon the Ring Tum Ditty over the halved potatoes and wait for the compliments.

PIRATES' HOUSE DEVILED CRAB

1	pound fresh crabmeat	⅓	cup mayonnaise
¾	cup cornbread crumbs	1	tablespoon Dijon mustard
¾	cup white bread crumbs		
1	medium onion, finely chopped	1	tablespoon lemon juice
1	bell pepper, finely chopped	2	tablespoons Worcestershire sauce
½	teaspoon pepper	½	teaspoon salt
2	ribs celery, finely chopped		Dash Tabasco sauce
2	eggs		

Combine crabmeat, bread crumbs, onion, pepper and celery in large bowl; beat together remaining ingredients until smooth. Mix well with crab. Pack into a shallow baking dish or a quiche dish is perfect. Bake at 350 degrees until hot, about 30 minutes.

Note: spare yourself and give your food processor a workout with crumbs, onion, pepper and celery. You may substitute white bread crumbs for cornbread. Serves 6.

FLOUNDER FLORENTINE

1	recipe Pepper Butter, (see below)	½	cup flour, seasoned with salt and pepper
3	bunches fresh spinach	1	recipe Blender Hollandaise Sauce, (see page 41)
6	4 to 5 ounce flounder filets, skinned		
1	pound large shrimp, peeled		

ADVANCED PREPARATION:

Make pepper butter. Stem and wash spinach carefully. Place in a large pot, do not add extra water. Cover pot and place over medium-high heat. Check after about 5 minutes and stir spinach gently. Lower heat and cook 3 to 4 more minutes, until spinach is just tender. Drain and reserve. Have shrimp peeled and flounder skinned. Have seasoned flour waiting on counter. Have ingredients for hollandaise sauce organized, 2 large skillets on the stove, and the oven on warm.

Have 6 dinner plates at the ready.

PEPPER BUTTER:

1	cup butter
1	clove garlic, finely chopped
1	tablespoon Worcestershire sauce
1	teaspoon Tabasco sauce
2	tablespoons black pepper
½	teaspoon crushed rosemary
1	teaspoon salt

TO ASSEMBLE:

Melt 2 tablespoons Pepper Butter in one skillet, sauté spinach until well-coated with butter. Turn heat off and cover. Melt 4 tablespoons Pepper Butter in the other skillet over medium-high heat; sauté shrimp, stirring frequently, until shrimp are pink and just done. Remove shrimp with slotted spoon, place in oven-proof dish and put in oven to keep warm. Melt 4 tablespoons Pepper Butter in same skillet over medium-high heat. Coat fish fillets lightly in seasoned flour and sauté 3 at a time (be careful not to crowd skillet) about 3 minutes to a side. Keep warm in oven with shrimp. Make hollandaise sauce. Divide spinach among dinner plates and place 1 filet on each pile of spinach. Place 5 or 6 shrimp on each filet. Cover each serving with 2 or 3 tablespoons hollandaise. Serve immediately. Serves 6.

Note: This recipe requires last minute preparation, but if you are organized, you can finish it off in 15 minutes.

SHRIMP IN PEPPER BUTTER

1	cup butter	1	teaspoon salt
1	clove garlic, finely chopped	2	tablespoons black pepper
1	teaspoon Tabasco sauce	½	teaspoon crushed
¼	cup Worcestershire sauce		rosemary
	Shrimp, unpeeled		

Melt butter; add remaining ingredients. Simmer for 10 minutes over very low heat, stirring often; mixture burns easily. Allow to congeal at room temperature, stirring occasionally before using. Store in refrigerator; warm to room temperature and stir up before using.

Note: Sauté large unpeeled shrimp in Pepper Butter. Serve with lots of French bread and lots of napkins. Count on ½ pound of shrimp per person.

Fun Fact: Tourism in Savannah has increased 46% since the publication of "The Book" as it is referred to locally. Thus, our shop "The Book" Gift Shop is the place to buy *Midnight in the Garden of Good and Evil* gifts and trivia.

Scallops Duxelles Savannah

2	pounds sea scallops		¼	cup water
½	small onion		¼	teaspoon thyme
¾	pound mushrooms			One sprig parsley
3	tablespoons butter			Small bay leaf
½	cup dry white wine		4	tablespoons butter
1	tablespoon lemon juice		1	cup heavy cream
2	teaspoons finely chopped			Pinch cayenne pepper
	fresh parsley		6	tablespoons freshly
4	tablespoons all-purpose flour			grated Parmesan
½	teaspoon salt			cheese, divided
¼	teaspoon nutmeg		½	teaspoon pepper
½	cup dry white wine			

Drop onion through feed tube of running food processor; chop fine. Add mushrooms, process until finely chopped, or chop very fine by hand. Melt 3 tablespoons butter in heavy skillet. Add mushrooms and onion; cook over medium heat, stirring occasionally, until liquid evaporates completely. Stir in ½ cup wine, lemon juice, chopped parsley, salt, pepper and nutmeg; cook, stirring occasionally, until wine evaporates completely. Set aside. In a large saucepan, heat ½ cup wine, water, thyme, sprig of parsley and bay leaf. Bring to a boil and add half the scallops. Simmer covered for 4 to 5 minutes, or until barely cooked. Remove with slotted spoon and repeat with remaining scallops, strain, reserving the broth. In a medium saucepan, melt 4 tablespoons butter, whisk in flour, then whisk in cream and add 1 cup of scallop broth. Cook over medium heat, stirring constantly, until sauce is thickened and comes to a boil. Correct seasoning. Combine ½ cup sauce with mushroom mixture. Add to remaining sauce 4 tablespoons Parmesan cheese and cayenne pepper to taste. Spread mushroom mixture on bottom of a 2-quart casserole. Arrange scallops on top. Pour sauce over scallops. Sprinkle with remaining 2 tablespoons Parmesan cheese and bake in a 400 degree oven for 15 minutes. Serves 6.

Note: Casserole may be prepared in advance and refrigerated before baking.

SEAFOOD AU GRATIN

1	pound crabmeat	Casserole sauce
1	pound cooked and peeled baby shrimp, (frozen are fine, but thaw them)	(see below)
½ to 1 cup grated Cheddar cheese		

Preheat oven to 350 degrees. Combine crabmeat, shrimp and casserole sauce. Pour into casserole dish. Top with grated cheese and bake until bubbly and cheese is melted, about 30 minutes.

Note: you may bake this in individual casseroles. Good with Savannah red rice, see recipe.

Serves 6 to 8.

CASSEROLE SAUCE

2	cups milk, divided	½	teaspoon salt
¼	cup all-purpose flour		Dash black pepper
½	cup Cheez Whiz		
½	cup grated Cheddar cheese		

Mix 1 ½ cups milk with cheese, Cheese Whiz, salt and pepper in a heavy saucepan; cook, stirring constantly, over medium heat until cheese melts and mixture boils. Mix ¼ cup flour with ½ cup milk until smooth. Stir into cheese mixture until thickened. Simmer for 20 minutes. If not using right away, place a piece of plastic wrap directly on surface of sauce to prevent a skin from forming.

Note: The Pirates' House uses this in their seafood au gratin, potatoes au gratin and as a sauce for broccoli.

CREOLE SHRIMP

1	recipe Creole Sauce, (see below)	1 to 2	pounds raw shrimp, peeled

When Creole Sauce is desired thickness, add shrimp and simmer until just cooked, about 5 minutes. Do not overcook shrimp. Serve on white rice or Savannah Red Rice (see recipe).
  Serves 6 to 8.

CREOLE SAUCE

¼	pound bacon, chopped	1	medium onion, chopped
3	ribs celery, chopped	1	bay leaf
1	clove garlic, crushed	1	teaspoon brown sugar
1	bell pepper, chopped	½	teaspoon black pepper
1	8 ounce bottle clam juice	1	teaspoon Tabasco sauce
1	cup chicken broth	1	teaspoon lemon juice
1	1 pound can tomato puree sauce		Dash Worcestershire sauce
1	tablespoon finely chopped fresh parsley		
1	tablespoon fresh or freeze-dried chives		

Fry bacon in a heavy pot. Add onion, garlic, celery and bell pepper and cook until onion is translucent. Add remaining ingredients, bring to a boil, lower heat and simmer uncovered, stirring occasionally, until sauce is thickened, 30 to 45 minutes.

PIRATES' HOUSE DUCK

2	5 pound Long Island ducklings, thawed	½	orange
	Salt and pepper		Soy sauce
2	teaspoons rosemary	¼	cup Grand Mariner or brandy
½	medium onion, peeled	1	recipe Orange Sauce for
½	apple		Duck (see below)

Remove insides of ducks; reserve livers and all available fat for Duck Liver Pate, (see recipe). Preheat oven to 350 degrees. Sprinkle insides of ducks with salt, pepper and 1 teaspoon of rosemary. Place ¼ onion, apple and orange in each cavity. Cut a slit in the tail and stick legs through to help duck hold shape. Fold neck skin under duck. Rub ducks all over with soy sauce and place breast-side down on a rack in a baking pan. Bake for 1 hour, turn breast-side up, and bake 1 ½ hours longer, or until skin is crisp and golden. Remove ducks from oven; let sit 15 minutes. Using kitchen shears, cut duck in half lengthwise down backbone. Discard backbone. Remove apple, orange and onion and discard. Place the 4 duck halves on an oven-proof serving platter. Run under broiler until crisp and hot, about 5 minutes. Meanwhile, warm liqueur carefully. Do not boil! Pour over ducks, turn out lights, ignite, and bring flaming ducks to the table amid oohs and aahs. Serve with Orange Sauce. Serves 4.

ORANGE DUCK SAUCE:

⅓	cup firmly packed light brown sugar	1	cup orange juice (including juice from oranges)
⅓	cup sugar		
	Grated rind of 1 orange	¼	teaspoon salt
	Rind of ½ orange, peeled so that no white is on rind and cut into very fine strips	1	tablespoon cornstarch
		1	tablespoon cold water

Combine sugars, grated orange rind and strips, orange juice and salt in a heavy saucepan. Bring to a boil, lower heat and simmer until strips of rind are tender, about 15 minutes. Dissolve cornstarch in cold water and add to sauce. Simmer, stirring constantly, until sauce thickens and becomes clear. May be made ahead and reheated gently.

Note: Keeps at least 1 month in the refrigerator.

CHATHAM ARTILLERY PUNCH

8	liters white rum	1	quart maraschino cherries, drained
4	liters gin		
4	liters rye	1	pound pineapple chunks, (fresh is best)
4	liters brandy		
3	gallons rose or Catawba wine	5	pounds light brown sugar Juice of 3 dozen lemons
1	pound green tea, steeped overnight in 2 gallons cold water and strained		Champagne

Mix all ingredients except champagne in a large, clean plastic trash can with lid. Cover and store in a cool place for a minimum of 2 months—it only improves with age. Serve in a punch bowl with a large block of ice. Add champagne to taste; 1 to 2 bottles per punch bowl. Also good mixed with orange juice and/or club soda for a lighter drink, or sipped straight as a liqueur. Make sure each cup contains some fruit, but by no means feed it to your children. This is the most subtly lethal punch you will ever drink. Three glasses and you're out!

Note: Perhaps you could make this a neighborhood project, or save your old wine bottles, bottle it, and give as Christmas presents. You say you don't want to make 10 gallons of punch? Oh, all right, here's a reduced version.

2	liters rum	2	cups maraschino cherries
1	liter gin	½	pound pineapple
1	liter rye	2 ½	cups firmly packed light brown sugar
1	liter brandy		
3	bottles rose or Catawba wine		Juice of 9 lemons
¼	pound green tea in 2 quarts cold water		

(Most Wal-Mart, Costco, Sam's or other stores like these sell 5 gallon buckets with lids; these are ideal to use).

PIRATES' HOUSE PUNCH

1   46 ounce can grapefruit juice
2   46 ounce cans pineapple juice
3   quarts orange juice
¾   cup maraschino cherry juice
       (or just enough to make a
       pinky-orange color)
1   bottle of ginger ale and/or
       orange sherbet balls
       Orange, lemon and lime slices
       for garnish

Mix first 4 ingredients together and chill. When ready to serve, add ginger ale and/or sherbet balls if desired. Garnish with sliced fruit.

Note: The maraschino cherry juice is imperative for the proper flavor. Have your friends save it for you if necessary. Freeze the punch mixture in a ring mold and use instead of ice in a punch bowl. Serve un-spiked to the kiddies and make yours into Pirates' Punch, see following recipe. Makes approximately 2 gallons.

PIRATES' PUNCH, A.K.A. SKULL CRUSHER

1   ounce rum   Pirates' House Punch,
1   ounce 151 rum   see previous recipe
½   ounce grenadine

Pour first 3 ingredients in large ice-filled glass mug or a skull mug is ideal. Top with punch. Stir. Garnish with orange, lime and cherry if desired.

Trivia: Which film features the interior and exterior of the Mercer House and is also the title of a chapter in "The Book?" (#30)

MRS. WILKES' BOARDING HOUSE

107 West Jones Street
Savannah, Georgia 31401
(912) 232-5997
(912) 233-8970 fax
www.mrswilkes.com

OPEN:
Monday-Friday
Lunch: 11am-2pm
CUISINE:
Home southern cooking
DRESS: Casual
OTHER: Catering

PRICE RANGE:
Lunch: $13
(1/2 price for children under 8)
CHARGE CARDS:
No
RESERVATIONS:
No

Dinner parties, by special arrangement

Ask anyone who was born in Savannah, or has lived here most of their life, where's a good place to go for lunch? They will more than likely mention, Mrs. Wilkes. Since the forties Mrs. Sema Wilkes (1907 - 2002) has owned or operated a dining room. Although she never intended opening a restaurant, she had always enjoyed preparing 'Family-style' meals for anyone who came in.

On November 24, 1965 Mrs. Wilkes purchased the now current Jones Street Boarding House and Dining Room. After a year of renovation the doors were open to the public and the same great food that was served back then is still served today.

When visiting Savannah make sure that if you are visiting Mrs. Wilkes, get there early and be prepared to wait. Once inside you will be seated at a dining table with other patrons, so make friends while you're in line.

Even though Mrs. Wilkes has passed on, the legend has not. The recipes and the secrets are now carried out by her family in the same tradition that Mrs. Wilkes started.

WILKES BOARDING HOUSE STYLE BISCUITS

2	cups self-rising flour	½	teaspoon baking powder
⅓	cup buttermilk	⅓	cup whole milk
1	tablespoon of Crisco		
2	tablespoons margarine (un-melted)		

Sift flour and baking powder into bowl. Cut in Crisco and margarine until mixture resembles coarse corn meal. Fill measuring cup with buttermilk, whole milk and enough water to make ¾ cup. Make well in center of dry flour, pour in liquid. With hands, mix lightly and quickly to form dough, moist enough to leave sides of bowl. Turn onto lightly floured surface. Knead by picking up sides of dough away from you pressing down with palms of hands, pushing dough away. Repeat 6 or 7 times. Work dough into large ball while kneading. Keep fingers dry by dipping into dry flour frequently. Pinch off portions of dough for desired size of biscuit. Press lightly to make biscuit appear flat and place on well greased pan. Bake in pre-heated oven at 450 degrees for 12 to 15 minutes. Makes approximately 16 biscuits.

CORNBREAD MUFFINS, SQUARES OR CRACKLIN' BREAD

1 ¼	cups corn meal	⅔	cup milk
¾	cup all-purpose flour (sifted)	⅓	cup salad oil
1	teaspoon salt	1	egg
1	teaspoon baking powder		

Mix liquid and dry ingredients separately. Pour mixed liquid into mixed dry ingredients. Stir with spoon until well mixed. Fill 12 greased muffin tins about ⅔ full. Bake in pre-heated oven for 25 minutes at 425 degrees. For squares bake same recipe in 8x8x2-inch pan. For cracklin' bread add 1 cup of pork fat cracklings to same basic recipe.

HUSH PUPPIES

2	cups plain meal	1	teaspoon pepper
1	cup self-rising flour	2	eggs
1	tablespoon baking powder	1	tablespoon catsup
2	tablespoons grated onion		Evaporated Milk
1	teaspoon salt		Water

Sift meal and flour together. Add all dry ingredients and onions. Beat in egg and catsup. Mix all other ingredients in and add equal amounts of evaporated milk and water until stiff batter is formed. Drop into hot oil by teaspoons. Dip spoon in water before returning to batter. Shake basket or turn until golden brown.

Trivia: Bobby Lee Cook called in what medical examiner as the first defense witness in the first trial and what other cases was this medical examiner working on at the time? (#61)

SHRIMP SALAD

1⅛	pound cooked, peeled, cleaned shrimp	½	cup mayonnaise
1	cup sliced celery	¼	cup sliced stuffed olives
½	cup chopped pickle or relish	¼	cup French dressing
½	teaspoon minced onion, (optional)		Salt and lemon juice to taste

Combine all ingredients in bowl. Chill or serve on lettuce, as a sandwich or with crackers.

MACARONI SALAD

1	pound elbow macaroni, cooked in salt until tender	2	boiled eggs
6	spring onions	1	small cucumber
1	tablespoon prepared mustard	1	diced fresh tomato
½	teaspoon black pepper	1	cup mayonnaise

Drain macaroni and rinse starch off. Toss with other ingredients. Chill.

Note: This is a favorite at Mrs. Wilkes.

Trivia: What was the testimony of a Candler emergency room nurse? In trying to help, what mistake did she make? (#31)

BACON CASSEROLE

½	pound bacon (cooked crisp)	¼	teaspoon pepper
2	tablespoons drippings	1	cup grated Swiss cheese
2	cups toasted bread crumbs	1	egg
2	tomatoes, peeled and sliced	1	cup milk
1	teaspoon salt	¼	teaspoon dry mustard

Crumble half of bacon slices with bread crumbs and drippings. Place in 1½ quart casserole dish. Add tomato slices. Combine seasoning and sprinkle on top. Top with grated cheese. Beat egg and milk together; pour over cheese. Bake 30 minutes at 350 degrees. Place remaining slices of bacon on top, bake an additional 5 to 8 minutes.

Yield: about 4 servings.

Whole canned tomatoes may be used. If you like tomatoes, add more than recipe suggest.

SQUASH CASSEROLE

4	pounds yellow squash	½	cup water
1	medium onion	½	stick margarine
1	teaspoon pepper	1	cup mushroom soup
1	tablespoon salt	1	cup grated American cheese

Slice squash and onion in saucepan. Cook in water over medium heat about 20 minutes. Drain in colander. Mash and add other ingredients except cheese, place in baking dish and cover top with grated cheese. Bake at 350 degrees for 20 minutes.

Trivia: What prompted Chablis to lead a "glittering procession" out of the Pickup and down Congress Street? (#34)

STEWED TOMATOES

2 ¼	teaspoons sugar (brown)	4	teaspoons butter or
4	teaspoons flour		margarine or bacon
1	#2 can or 2 ½ cups		drippings
	quartered, peeled tomatoes		Pepper to taste
1	teaspoon minced onion (optional)		
1	teaspoon salt		

Mix sugar with flour; add rest of ingredients. Simmer 10 minutes.
  Makes 4 servings.

FRIED EGGPLANT

Pare large eggplant; cut into ¼ -inch crosswise ties. Sprinkle with salt, pepper, and flour. If preferred you can dip into beaten egg, then into cracker crumbs. In hot bacon fat or salad oil, fry eggplant until golden brown on both sides—about 6 to 8 minutes. Serve with catsup or chili sauce.

SUCCOTASH

1 ½	cups hot cooked or canned whole-kernel corn	1 ½	cups hot cooked or canned green, limas or shell beans
2	tablespoons butter or margarine		
½	cup light cream		Salt and pepper, to taste

Combine all ingredients, adding salt and pepper. Heat.
  Makes 6 servings.

FRIED CHICKEN

2 ½   pounds fryer, cut up and sprinkled with salt
        and pepper
2   tablespoons evaporated milk
2   tablespoons water

Pour over chicken ingredients above and marinate for about 10 minutes. Dip chicken in bowl of all-purpose flour. Shake off excess flour. Deep fry in Wesson oil at 300 degrees or pan fry on medium (making sure oil is hot before putting chicken in). Make sure chicken is covered with oil at all times. Fry until golden brown.

CHICKEN AND DUMPLINGS

2 ½ pounds chicken, disjointed and ready to cook

Cover with water in saucepan, sprinkle with one teaspoon salt and one teaspoon pepper. Boil over medium heat for 30 minutes. Pour off broth, (use for dumplings).

DUMPLINGS

2   cups all-purpose flour
½   cup milk
½   cup water

Mix in bowl and knead into another bowl of flour until dough is firm. Mash flat on floured surface. Let stand about 10 minutes. Roll out with rolling pin until knife blade thin. Cut into 2" squares. Drop into boiling broth (that you, hopefully, saved from above). Cook about 10 minutes on high heat. Reduce heat to low and return chicken to pot. Pour in 1 ½ cups of milk into mixture and stir. Remove from heat. Add salt and pepper if needed.

MEAT LOAF

2	cups corn flakes (crushed)	2	tablespoons soy sauce
¾	cup minced onion	2 ½	teaspoons salt
¼	cup minced green pepper	1	tablespoon mustard
2	eggs	¼	cup milk
2	pounds ground chuck	1	can mushroom soup

Preheat oven to 400 degrees. With fork, beat eggs, slightly.

Lightly mix in meat, crumbs, onions and pepper. Combine other ingredients. The secret is to mix well but lightly. Do not pack. In baking dish, shape meat into oval loaf. Bake for 50 minutes at 350 degrees, or until done.

BEEF STEW

3 pounds boneless stew (or short ribs of beef) and 1 large sliced onion. Cut meat into serving size portions. Sprinkle each piece with salt and pepper. Cook in heavy pot on top of stove. Add enough water to cover bottom of pot. Put lid on pot. When meat is cooking well, remove top of pot while cooking on medium heat. Let meat cook in its own juices. Turn meat with fork until brown. Return lid to pot and cook about 1 hour on low heat. Check frequently, if juices are cooking out then add some water. When meat is fork tender, add about 2 tablespoons flour to water and pour over meat. Stir well. If broth becomes too thick, add more water. Simmer until ready to serve.

This is a wonderful Beef Stew and should be served hot with your favorite vegetables. If there are any leftovers, I like to have a meat sandwich the next day (hot or cold).

Trivia: Who accompanied Jackie Onassis on her trip to Savannah? (#21)

CHICKEN PIE

1	fryer, cooked and cubed	3	cups of chicken broth
½	pint half and half	3	boiled eggs, sliced
	fresh cream		Salt and pepper to taste

Combine fryer, half and half, chicken broth and salt and pepper. Slice eggs over this after placing in 9x12-inch pan. Pour crust (see below) over mixture. Do not stir. Bake at 425 degrees for 45 minutes to 1 hour or until crust is brown.

CRUST

¾	cup melted butter	1 ½	teaspoons baking powder
1 ½	cups milk	1 ½	cups self-rising flour

Mix all ingredients and pour over chicken.

COUNTRY STYLE STEAK

Trim edges of fat off steaks and pound meat with neck of cola bottle. Sprinkle generously with salt, pepper and dash of garlic powder. Dip meat in flour and shake. Fry in oil quickly until brown but not cooked too much inside. This is done by cooking both sides on high heat, turning quickly and then reducing heat to low to finish cooking.

Boil ½ cup minced onion in another pot with ¼ cup water, for about 5 minutes. When finished cooking as many steaks as desired, leave about 3 tablespoons browned crumbs (not burned) and fat from steak in skillet. Add onion and 3 tablespoons flour. Stir until slightly browned. Slowly pour in 3 cups hot water as it thickens. Add salt and pepper to taste. Gravy may be served over rice or over steaks.

PINEAPPLE UPSIDE-DOWN CAKE

1 ½	cups flour	1	egg
1	cup sugar	1	stick margarine
2	teaspoons baking powder	1	cup brown sugar
½	teaspoon salt	1	can sliced pineapple
⅓	cup butter		(drained)
⅔	cup milk		Maraschino cherries
1	teaspoon vanilla		

Melt butter (1 stick) in oblong pan. Top with brown sugar; pineapple slices and cherries. Stir flour, sugar, baking powder and salt together. Add butter, milk and flavoring. Beat 2 minutes at medium speed, add egg and beat 2 more minutes. Pour batter over pineapple slices and bake at 350 degrees for 30 to 35 minutes.

FRESH STRAWBERRY PIE

1	quart strawberries	2	tablespoons lemon juice
1	cup sugar	1	baked pie shell
2 ½ - 3 tablespoons cornstarch		½	pint whipping cream

Wash berries and hull. Put one half of berries in saucepan and crush. Mix sugar and cornstarch; add to crushed berries along with lemon juice. Cook on medium heat until mixture thickens. Cool. Cut remaining berries into halves and mix with the cooked mixture. Add a few drops of red food coloring to the cooked mixture before adding the uncooked berries. Chill before serving. Serve topped with whipped cream.

Trivia: What is something distinguishable Minerva wears? (#23)

17 Hundred 90 Inn and Restaurant

307 E. President Street
Savannah, Georgia 31401
(912) 236-7122
Website: www.17hundred90.com
Chef: Robert Bruso
Restaurant Hours:
Lunch (weekdays only): 11:30 - 2:00 pm
Dinner nightly: 6:00 - 10:00 pm

The restaurant located inside 17 Hundred and 90 has been the host to local's and travelers alike for years. Many restaurants boast of the fine dining experience you will have, but deliver only pretension and price. At 17 Hundred 90 you are guaranteed wonderful entrées, professional service, and an elegant setting in which to enjoy your evening out.

The restaurant is tastefully decorated in old southern tradition from the perfectly restored fireplaces to the brick floors throughout. We hope that your experience at 17 Hundred 90 will compliment your memories for years to come and remain a highlight of your stay in the wonderful historic city of Savannah.

CRAB CAKES

2	pounds crab claw meat
½	red pepper
½	green bell pepper
2	eggs
½	ounce seafood seasoning
¼	red onion
1	cup bread crumbs
½	cup mayonnaise (or until moist)
1	tablespoon Worcestershire sauce

Dice all vegetables; add all ingredients together, except bread crumbs, and mix until moist and make nice firm cakes. Form cake patties.

When you are ready to serve, coat crab cakes with bread crumbs and pan seer them with olive oil over medium heat until golden brown, then bake in oven until hot; then serve.

CHICKEN MARSALA

1	8 ounce breast of chicken
4	ounces of crimini mushrooms
2	ounces of Mondovi or Marsala wine
	Butter
	Olive oil
	Flour
	Salt and pepper to taste

Coat the chicken in flour and pan seer over medium heat until golden brown. Bake chicken in oven at 400 degrees until fully cooked, about 6 to 8 minutes. While the chicken is cooking, you can make the sauce. Sauté mushrooms with a little olive oil and salt and pepper until soft and cooked through. De-glaze pan with wine and let reduce by half.

Once reduced, add a little butter to your demi-glaze and pour over chicken; serve hot.

INNS OF SAVANNAH
AND THE
LOW COUNTRY

Gazebo Romance Garden © 1988 Sharon Saseen

FINEST AND BEST
OF THE BEST

Pamela Lee

BALLASTONE INN BED & BREAKFAST

Fourteen East Oglethorpe Avenue
Savannah, Georgia USA 31401-3707
A first in Savannah Georgia Luxury ...
Luxury Bed and Breakfast Inn
(912) 236-1484 (800) 822-4553 (912)236-4626 Fax
Email: Inn@ballastone.com Web: www.ballastone.com

Chef Charlotte

In recognition of The Savannah Georgia Hotel's historical significance, the Ballastone Inn of Savannah has been awarded two commemorative plaques, one from the Historic Savannah Foundation and one from the National Trust. It is truly an historic hotel. The land where the hotel is situated formed part of the southern boundary of the original settlement founded by General James E. Oglethorpe in the fall of 1733.

The building recaptured its former respectability in 1940 when it was converted into 18 modern apartments to house "indispensable immigrant war workers," as the new tenants were described in the news of that day. At the close of World War II, the building became the York

Apartments and began a slow deterioration during the late 40's and 50's, which mirrored the decline of the surrounding neighborhood.

In April of 1969, the Girl Scouts of America purchased the property and refurbished the building's lower level for use as administrative offices. In 1980, the old building was sold to private owners and was converted into a modern bed-and-breakfast inn, one of the first in the famed historic district and the precursor of the historic Savannah Hotel and comfort. It is the first Savannah bed and breakfast inn, not just another Savannah hotel. In June 2002, after six months of planning, an Atlanta couple, Jennifer, a native Georgian, and Jim Salandi, purchased the hotel. Focus will be on elegance and formality for the uniquely intimate Ballastone.

BLUEBERRY CREAM CHEESE FRENCH TOAST

1	loaf French Bread	6	eggs
1	cup blueberries, (frozen are fine)	1 ½	cups milk
8	ounces cream cheese	⅓	cup maple syrup

Slice enough French bread to fit into the bottom of a 9 x 13 pan. Cut remaining bread into small cubes. Spread sliced bread with cream cheese. Sprinkle blueberries on top of bread; add bread cubes on top of blueberries.

Beat together eggs, milk, and syrup. Pour over bread cubes.

Cover with foil that has been sprayed with Pam. Refrigerate overnight. Bake at 350 degrees-30 minutes covered and 30 minutes uncovered.

Serve with blueberry sauce.

BLUEBERRY SAUCE

1	cup blueberries	1	cup sugar
1	cup water	3	tablespoons cornstarch

Boil together until thickened. Serves 12.

CHARLOTTE'S STUFFED BAGUETTE

1	cup grated Swiss cheese	1	cup Parmesan cheese
1	stick		butter, softened
½	cup chopped blond		pistachio nuts
1	loaf French bread		

In a medium sized bowl or food processor, mix the cheeses and butter until well blended. The mixture should be a thick paste. If it is too thick, add a little heavy cream. Stir in the pistachios. Slice the bread crosswise into 3 or 4 sections and pull out the soft insides. Stuff the cavities with the cheese mixture. Reform the bread into a single loaf, wrap in foil or plastic wrap and chill for at least 2 hours.

When you are ready to serve, slice the loaf into ½ inch slices.

PECAN CORNBREAD

⅔	cup ground pecans	⅓	cup butter, melted
⅔	cup flour	½	cup buttermilk
⅔	cup yellow cornmeal	2	eggs
½	cup sugar	¾	teaspoon baking powder
½	teaspoon baking soda		

Stir together dry ingredients.Mix all wet ingredients together and add to dry ingredients. Spoon into 10 inch pie plate-batter is very thick.

Bake at 400 degrees for 25 minutes. Serves 10-12.

THE BEAUFORT INN

809 Port Republic Street
Beaufort, South Carolina 29902
(843) 521-9000
(843) 521-9500 Fax
website: www.beaufortinn.com

Keith A. Josefiak, Executive Chef

The Beaufort Inn is within easy walking distance to numerous historic attractions, museums, galleries, restaurants, Beaufort's award-winning Waterfront Park and Marina. The Beaufort Inn offers unsurpassed accommodations and AAA Four Diamond dining.

Guests of The Beaufort Inn are welcomed with classic Southern hospitality, style and comfort. Heart-pine floors, fireplaces, cast-iron soaking tubs and a multitude of porches are just a few of the features that distinguish The Beaufort Inn.

All guest rooms are uniquely decorated in a classic style that compliments the history of the Inn, but also offer modern-day amenities. You may stay in a room with large picture windows, king-size bed, fireplace, wet bar and convertible sofa. Or you may choose to look out over historic downtown Beaufort from the bay windows of your room.

Private gardens and intimate courtyards connect you to charming cottage suites, offering king-size beds and large bathrooms with soaking tubs and separate showers.

The Beaufort Inn is also home to a celebrated restaurant. Rated Four Diamonds by AAA, the Veranda Restaurant offers the area's finest cuisine. The restaurant is a favorite among locals and worldwide travelers for its exceptional dishes, such as our Lowcountry Bouillabaisse.

We invite you to experience a classic Southern inn in a historic Southern town. Our superior service, outstanding dining and accommodations will greatly exceed your expectations, and you will see for yourself why The Beaufort Inn is *"Where History is Made."*

DROP BISQUITS

2   cups all-purpose flour
1   tablespoon baking powder
1   teaspoon salt
½   teaspoon black pepper
½   cup (4 ounces) Crisco shortening
¾   cup shredded Cheddar cheese
2   scallions, trimmed and minced
1   tablespoon parsley, minced
1+ cups half and half

In a Kitchen Aid type mixing bowl, with paddle attachment; combine the flour, baking powder, salt and black pepper. Mix just to combine. Add the shortening, mix until crumbly. Add the cheddar cheese, scallions and parsley. While on low speed, slowly add the half & half and mix until combined. The mixture should be wet to the touch. **Do not over mix**. Spoon onto parchment lined baking sheet. Bake in a preheated 375 degree oven until golden brown, about 12-15 minutes.

Yields about 12-15 biscuits.

SPINACH, ESCAROLE & RADICCHIO SALAD

Kumquats, Red Onions and Citrus Vinaigrette

1	small can frozen 5-ALIVE juice concentrate
2	tablespoons ginger, peeled and minced
	Saffron, pinch, (optional)
1	tablespoon Dijon mustard
2	tablespoons raspberry vinegar
1	cup vegetable / olive oil blend
	Salt to taste
¾	pound baby spinach, washed and dried
1	small head radicchio, cored, chiffonade and washed
1	head escarole, torn and washed
½	cup shaved red onion, rinsed
½	pint kumquats, sliced and seeded
	Fresh cracked black pepper
1	cup almond slivers, toasted

In a small saucepan, combine the 5-Alive, ginger and saffron. Bring to a simmer over medium heat and reduce by half, about 10 minutes. Transfer to a blender and add the raspberry vinegar and mustard. Puree until smooth. While blending, slowly add the oil blend. Strain through a fine sieve and season to taste with salt. Reserve and chill.

In a large salad bowl, combine the spinach, radicchio, escarole and red onions. Toss until well combined and divide onto serving dishes and garnish with kumquats and almonds.

Serves 4-6.

SEARED SCALLOP & OYSTER STEW

2	tablespoons olive oil	2	shallots, finely chopped
1	cup dry white wine	1	dried pasilla pepper,
1	cup heavy cream		stemmed, seeded and
2	cups clam juice		crumbled
1	roasted red pepper,	1	roasted yellow pepper,
	peeled, seeded, small dice		peeled, seeded, small dice
½	pound large scallops	12	oysters, shucked,
	Salt to taste		reserving oyster juice
	White pepper to taste	1	tablespoon fresh
1	tablespoon parsley,		tarragon, chopped
	chopped		

In a medium saucepan heat 1 tablespoon of the olive oil over high heat, add the shallots and cook until tender. Add the wine and reduce by ½. Once reduced, add the heavy cream and reduce by ⅓, about 5 minutes. Remove from heat and add the crumbled pasilla peppers and allow to steep for 10 minutes.

In a medium saucepan, over high heat, reduce the clam and oyster juices by ½. Meanwhile, place the pepper/cream mixture into a blender and puree until smooth. Strain through a fine sieve into the clam juice pan while discarding pasilla scraps. Adjust the seasoning of the broth to taste with salt and white pepper. Keep warm over low heat.

Heat a large Teflon-coated sauté pan over high heat and add remaining olive oil. Season the scallops with salt and white pepper. Carefully add the scallops to hot pan, allowing them not to overlap. Cook until well seared, about 2-3 minutes. Quickly turn the scallops and cook until desire doneness. Add the oysters and peppers and cook until the oysters are heated through.

Meanwhile, return the pasilla broth to a boil. Equally divide the scallops, peppers and oysters among 4 hot soup bowls. Carefully ladle the hot broth into the bowls. Sprinkle with chopped tarragon and parsley and serve. Serves 4 as a first course, 2 as an entree.

THE GINGERBREAD HOUSE

1921 Bull Street
Savannah, Georgia 31401
(912) 234-7303
Website: www.thegingerbreadhouse.net

The Gingerbread House is considered one of the most outstanding examples of Steamboat Gothic gingerbread carpentry in the United States. When the home was built by the Asendorf family in 1899, people in Savannah soon began calling it The Gingerbread House because of the elaborate gingerbread arches and spindles adorning the front porches and side balcony of the house.

Through the years, the home has been visited by many celebrities. President Woodrow Wilson's wife, a native of Savannah, wanted to purchase the home, and it was said to be President Eisenhower's favorite house in the area. President Roosevelt even stopped the 1933 bicentennial parade so he and his mother could view the home more closely.

For two decades, Savannah's most photographed house has been the setting for many special occasions, from large wedding receptions to elegant dinner parties. The home has also been a favorite stop for tour groups, providing services ranging from a tour of the home with refreshments to private seated dinners and cocktail parties.

This lovely home will satisfy even the most discerning tastes. An exquisite interior of understated elegance is highlighted by Victorian furniture and appointments and pink marble baths. A large, enclosed conservatory provides an informal complement to the original interior. The conservatory opens into a beautifully landscaped courtyard complete with formal plantings, pond and waterfall, a gazebo, and herb garden.

BACON BREAD STICKS

1 package Italian bread sticks   1 pound bacon
   Parmesan cheese

Cut bacon strips in half. Dredge bacon in cheese and wrap around bread sticks with cheese on inside. Place on microwave pan, cover with paper towel and cook about 8 at a time on high, 3 ½ to 4 minutes. Drain on paper towel; roll in additional cheese while warm. Serve at room temperature.
Makes approximately 24.

PRALINE CHEESECAKE

1 ¼	cups graham crumbs	1	5 ⅓ ounce can evaporated milk	
¼	cup granulated sugar			
¼	cup finely chopped pecans, toasted	2	tablespoons all-purpose flour	
1 ½	teaspoons vanilla	¼	cup butter or margarine, melted	
3	eggs			
½	cup pecan halves, toasted	3	8 ounce packages cream cheese, softened	
1	cup dark corn syrup			
¼	cup cornstarch	1	cup brown sugar	
1	teaspoon vanilla	2	tablespoons brown sugar	

Combine crumbs, sugar and pecans. Stir in butter; press mixture over bottom and sides of a 9-inch spring form pan. Bake in a 350 degree oven 10 minutes. In a large bowl, combine cream cheese and 1 cup brown sugar. Add milk, flour and 1 ½ teaspoons vanilla; beat well. Add eggs; beat until blended. Pour into crust. Bake at 350 degrees for 50 minutes or until set. Cool 30 minutes; loosen sides, remove rim from pan and cool. Arrange pecan halves over cheesecake; spoon sauce over nuts.

SAUCE:

Combine syrup, cornstarch and remaining brown sugar in saucepan. Cook and stir until thickened and bubbly; cook and stir 2 minutes more. Remove from heat; stir in remaining vanilla, cool slightly; stir before serving.

Serves 16.

Note: I hope that you will love this as much as I do. We had our daughter, Stephanie's graduation party at The Gingerbread House. It's a lovely place for a party or reception. Herbert, his wife and daughter truly know Southern courtesy and hospitality. Thank You.

GRANITE STEPS

Granite Steps (a former Bed & Breakfast) is now closed, but not forgotten. Its allure and grandeur makes it one of the most desirable mansions in Savannah. This home is located at 126 East Gaston Street, one block behind "The Book" Gift Shop. It was the last home that Jim Williams refurbished. The Married Women's Card Club was filmed here for "The Movie."

GRANITE STEPS COUNTRY BLUEBERRY COFFEE CAKE

½	cup packed light brown sugar	1	cup quick-cooking rolled oats
½	teaspoon cinnamon	1 ½	cups fresh or frozen blueberries
½	cup (1 stick) butter, melted, plus 2 tablespoons cut into small pieces	1	12 ounce can Pillsbury Big Country buttermilk biscuits

Preheat oven to 375 degrees. Generously grease a 9-inch square baking dish. In a small bowl, combine brown sugar and cinnamon and mix well with a fork. Separate biscuit dough into 10 biscuits. Cut each biscuit into quarters, and dip each piece in melted butter and coat with brown sugar mixture. Arrange in a single layer in baking dish. Sprinkle with ½ cup of the oats. Combine blueberries and granulated sugar in a bowl and toss to coat; spoon over oats and biscuits and sprinkle with remaining ½ cup of oats. Top with butter pieces. Bake for 30 to 35 minutes or until cake is golden brown and center is done. Cool for 20 minutes. Serve warm.

French Toast Stuffed with Bananas and Walnuts

Sandwiching two slices of bread with a mixture of bananas and walnuts results in French toast with a surprise filling. Try other favorite nuts in place of the walnuts, if you like. Accompany the French toast with bacon, ham or sausage.

6	eggs	8	slices egg bread
¼	cup milk	¼	cup (1 ounce) coarsely
4	very ripe bananas		chopped walnuts
4	tablespoons (½ stick)		Confectioners' sugar,
	unsalted butter		for dusting
⅛	teaspoon freshly grated nutmeg		

In a large, shallow bowl, using a fork, beat eggs until lightly frothy. Stir in the milk; set aside. Peel the bananas into a small bowl and mash them with a fork. Stir in the walnuts and the nutmeg. Spread the banana-walnut mixture evenly over half the bread slices, leaving a ¼-inch border uncovered on all edges. Top with the remaining bread slices and press down gently to seal. Place 2 sandwiches in the egg mixture and press down gently. Turn gently and let soak for a moment, until evenly saturated on both sides. Remove from the bowl and repeat with the remaining 2 sandwiches. In a frying pan or on a griddle large enough to hold all the sandwiches at once, melt 2 tablespoons of the butter over medium heat. Add the sandwiches and fry until the undersides are golden brown, about 2 minutes. Cut the remaining 2 tablespoons butter into several pieces and dot them around the pan. Flip the sandwiches with a spatula and fry until the second side is browned, about 2 minutes longer. Place the French toast on warmed individual plates. Using a small, fine sieve, lightly dust the tops with confectioners' sugar. Serve hot, with jam or maple syrup.
  Serves 4.

Oven-Baked Dutch Apple Pancakes

2   cans apple pie filing
2   tablespoons butter
1   teaspoon cinnamon
3   eggs
½   cup milk

½   cup all-purpose flour
1   tablespoon sour cream
1   teaspoon lemon zest
¼   teaspoon salt
     Confectioners' sugar, for dusting

Preheat oven to 350 degrees. In a 10-inch cast-iron skillet, warm the apple pie filing, butter, and cinnamon. In a bowl, beat the eggs until frothy. Add the milk, flour, sour cream, lemon zest, and salt. Beat just until the batter is smooth. Pour over the hot apple mixture in the skillet, and immediately put the pan in the oven. Bake for 20 to 25 minutes, or until the pancake is puffed and golden brown. Using a small, fine sieve, lightly dust the top of the pancake with confectioners' sugar. Serve warm.

Serves 4-6.

THE GASTONIAN

220 East Gaston Street
Savannah, Georgia 31401
(912) 232-2869
(800) 322-6603
www.BedandBreakfastsofSavannah.com

The Gastonian, comprised of two striking Regency-Italianate style mansions, rests in the heart of Savannah's beautiful Historic District. Built in 1868, the mansions served as a residence until 1985. These majestic mansions, like many of Savannah's old homes, serve as reminders of Savannah's rich history.

The exterior cracks along the mansions' facade and a crack along the fireplace in the original kitchen of The Gastonian were caused by an earthquake that struck the Coastal Empire in the late 1800s. Many Savannahians fled their homes during the panic, but The Gastonian remained standing.

In December of 2000, The Gastonian was selected for membership in Relais & Chateaux, the international association of luxury hotels and restaurants. Membership in this very elite group distinguished The Gastonian as one of the finest luxury hotels in the world.

On April 1, 2005, HLC Hotels, Inc, a Savannah-owned and operated hotel management company, purchased The Gastonian and added it to its downtown collection of upscale historic inns in Savannah, including The Marshall House, The Eliza Thompson House, The East Bay Inn and The Olde Harbour Inn. The Gastonian is now the leading historic inn in the collection.

Buttermilk Peach Pecan Pancakes

3	fresh eggs
¾	teaspoon salt
3	cups buttermilk
1	tablespoon baking soda
¾	teaspoon pure vanilla extract
1	tablespoon baking powder
¼	cup corn oil
⅛	cup quick oats
4	cups all-purpose flour
¾	cup fresh Georgia Peach slices
2	tablespoons sugar
½	cup Georgia Pecan pieces

Mix together eggs, buttermilk, vanilla and corn oil; set aside. In a separate large bowl, mix together flour, sugar, salt, baking soda, baking powder, quick oats, sliced peaches, and pecans. Add wet ingredients until just combined. Let mixture stand for 20 minutes before cooking. Cook on griddle, flipping pancakes when they start to bubble. Serve hot with real maple syrup.

Strawberry Soup

1	quart strawberries, hulled	⅔	cup sour cream
4	cups buttermilk	3	tablespoons peach
¾	cup sugar		schnapps
	Fresh mint sprigs		

In the bowl of a food processor, combine the strawberries, 1 cup of the buttermilk, and the sugar; process until blended and set aside. Combine the remaining 3 cups of buttermilk, the sour cream, and schnapps in a large bowl. Pour the strawberry mixture into the sour cream mixture and stir to combine. Cover and refrigerate until well chilled. Serve the soup chilled in small cups, garnished with mint sprigs.

PESTO, GOAT CHEESE & SUN-DRIED TOMATO TORTE

1	cup coarsely chopped fresh basil
1	cup coarsely chopped spinach
1 ½	teaspoons minced garlic
¼	cup virgin olive oil
1	cup Parmesan cheese
	Ground black pepper to taste
8	ounces cream cheese
4	ounces goat cheese
⅓	cup sun-dried tomato paste
¼	cup chopped fine nuts (optional)

Chop basil, spinach and garlic in food processor. While machine is running, gradually add olive oil through feed tube. Add parmesan cheese and process until almost smooth. Season with pepper; set aside. Blend cream cheese and goat cheese in a medium bowl until smooth.

Line a 3-cup bowl with plastic wrap; leave a 4-inch overhang. Mold the pesto into a disk and distribute evenly in bottom of prepared bowl. Spread goat cheese/cream cheese mixture on top of pesto and finish with the sun-dried tomato paste. Fold plastic overhang over top and refrigerate.

Approximately 30 minutes before serving, unfold plastic wrap and invert onto serving plate. Serve at room temperature. Freezes well.

SCONE MIX

4	cups flour	½	cup plus
2	tablespoons sugar	½	teaspoon salt
1	tablespoon baking powder	½	pound butter
1	cup heavy cream	1	cup milk

Combine all dry ingredients. Cube the butter and mix together. Add the remaining wet ingredients and mix only until combined. Do not over mix. Roll out dough approximately 1 inch thick and press with biscuit cutter. Bake at 380 degrees for about 5 minutes or until brown.

Note: For a variety, add your choice of nuts, chocolate chips, dried fruit, poppy seed or coconut to basic mix.

TRADITIONAL RAISIN SCONES

3	cups all-purpose flour	3	large eggs
1	tablespoon baking powder	⅓	cup buttermilk
1	cup (2 sticks) unsalted butter at room temperature	½	cup raisins
		¼	cup, plus 2 tablespoons sugar

Preheat the oven to 350 degrees. Sift together the flour and baking powder. In a separate bowl, beat the butter until creamy. Add the ¼ cup sugar, beating until pale and fluffy. Add the eggs, one at a time; add the flour mixture and the buttermilk. Sprinkle the raisins over the dough and gently fold them in. Using an ice cream scoop, place mounds of dough on a baking sheet and sprinkle with the remaining sugar. Bake for 30 minutes. Serve the scones warm, with softened butter and preserves.

Yields 1 Dozen Scones.

ALMOND SKILLET CAKE

¾   cup of butter or margarine
1-½   cups of sugar
2   eggs
1-½   cups sifted all-purpose flour
       Pinch of salt
1   tablespoon almond flavor
       Sliced almonds
       Sugar

Melt butter then add to sugar in a large mixing bowl. Mix well. Beat in eggs one at a time. Add the flour, salt, and almond flavoring. Mix well. Line an iron skillet with aluminum foil letting the foil hang over the sides. Put the batter in the skillet. Cover with sliced almonds and sprinkle with sugar. Bake for 40 minutes at 350 degrees. Remove from the skillet when cool. DO NOT SLICE UNTIL THE NEXT DAY.

ELIZA THOMPSON HOUSE

5 West Jones Street
Savannah, Georgia 31401
(800) 348-9378 Reservations
(912) 236-3620
(912) 238-1920 Fax
innkeeper@elizathompsonhouse.com

Eliza Thompson built her fabulous home in 1847, a prosperous time in Savannah where elegant parties in fine homes were popular. Today, the Eliza Thompson House is one of the City's oldest and most elegant bed and breakfast inns.

This award-winning Inn is located on historic Jones Street, one of Savannah's most charming downtown addresses. The Inn is within walking distance to shops, antique stores, museum houses, civil war memorials, beautiful old churches and Savannah's finest restaurants.

The Eliza Thompson House consists of 12 rooms in the "Main House" and 13 rooms in Eliza's own "Carriage House," which overlooks the courtyard. Each guestroom is tastefully and uniquely furnished with period furnishings and modern amenities. Each has a private bath.

In February 2001, HLC Hotels, Inc., a Savannah-owned and operated hotel management company, purchased the Eliza Thompson House and added it to its downtown collection of upscale historic inns in Savannah, including The Marshall House, East Bay Inn and Olde Harbour Inn. Visit all five inns at: www. BedandBreakfastofSavannah.com

BAKED BRIE WITH ALMONDS

1   **9-inch refrigerated pie crust**
1   **small round brie**
4-5 **tablespoons peach preserves**
       Sliced almonds, place a few aside
       for topping

Preheat oven to 350 degrees. Slice brie in half (through the middle) and place one half in center of the crust. Spread a small amount of preserves on top of the brie and then place the second half of the brie on top. Spread another layer of preserves on top of the second half and sprinkle with the almonds. Fold the pie crust around the brie, pinching edges together. Top with additional almonds. Bake for 20 minutes or until crust is golden brown.

CRAB SPREAD

½   pound canned crabmeat *
⅓   cup lemon or lime juice
3   ounces cream cheese
¼   cup mayonnaise
3   tablespoons green onion, finely chopped
⅛   tablespoon garlic salt

Mix crab and lemon or lime juice and let sit one hour. Drain well in a sieve. Mix with other ingredients.

* If you cannot find crabmeat, you may purchase it from "The Book" Gift Shop at (912) 233-3867.

ARTICHOKE DIP

1   8 ½ ounce can or jar artichoke hearts, drained
1   cup Parmesan cheese
1   cup mayonnaise
¼   tablespoon lemon juice
     Dash Tabasco sauce
     Dash garlic powder
     Dash paprika

Preheat oven to 325 degrees. Drain artichoke and mash with a fork, or use food processor. Add cheese and mayonnaise and mix well. Add lemon juice, Tabasco sauce, and garlic powder. Sprinkle with paprika. Put in a shallow casserole or pie dish. Bake for 30 minutes.

NOGS

Green Meldrim Gardens © 1998 Sharon Saseen

THOSE "TRUE" SAVANNAHIANS THAT CHOOSE TO STAY NORTH OF GASTON STREET

"Midnight" Martini

(In memory of Pinkie Masterpoulos,
Pinkie Masters)

Equal parts of Bourbon, Gin, and orange liqueur; stir and strain into martini glass and garnish with a cherry.

Pinkie Masters Lounge
318 Drayton Street
Savannah, Georgia 31401
(912) 238-0447

NOGS Martini

2	parts Amaretto
1	part almond Schnapps

Mix in pitcher of ice, strain; pour into martini glasses and garnish with 2 whole almonds in each glass.

Trivia: Why was it good to have Wanda Brooks at Emma's?
(#37)

NOGS: Those "True" Savannahians

GIRL SCOUT PUNCH

(From the kitchen of Margaret Debolt)

1	12 ounce can frozen orange juice concentrate, thawed in refrigerator	1	cup apricot nectar, chilled
½	cup lemon juice, chilled	½	cup light corn syrup
3	12 ounce cans ginger ale, chilled		Cold Water
			Orange, lemon, or lime slices for garnish (optional)

Mix orange juice with three juice cans of cold water. Add other juices and syrup. Pour over block of ice in chilled punch bowl; stir in ginger ale. Garnish with fruit slices if desired.

CHABLIS' HOT ASPARAGUS DIP

2	15 ounce cans asparagus, cut spears	1	clove garlic, crushed
1 ¼	cups mayonnaise		Salt and red pepper
½	cup sour cream		Dash of pepper
1 ⅔	cups freshly grated Parmesan cheese	¼	teaspoon Tabasco sauce

Drain asparagus, then mash up in a mixing bowl; add remaining ingredients, mixing together well. Pour into baking dish and bake for 20-30 minutes at 350 degrees or until slightly brown and bubbling. Serve hot with crackers (also good with seasoned bagel chips).

Trivia: Where did Chablis perform? (#17)

MANDY'S BRIE IN PASTRY

2	4 ounce packages brie	4	frozen Pepperidge Farms
	Brown sugar		pastry shells
	Butter		Walnuts, chopped

Roll out two of the pastry shells into a thin pastry. Cut out 8-inch circle and wrap with cheese and pat of butter. Sprinkle with brown sugar and a sprinkle of chopped walnuts; seal edges. Place each pastry on an un-greased baking sheet in a 400 degree oven for 20-25 minutes or until pastry is brown. You may decorate and design cheese with remaining pastry. Serve hot with crackers.

Note: When Deborah was a partner at the Hamilton-Turner Mansion, they would serve this with crackers and a huge fruit tray.

VIDALIAS AND SWISS CHEESE
(From the kitchen of Margaret Debolt)

4	large Vidalia onions, cut in chunks
¼	cup butter
1	cup rice, cooked
1	cup Swiss cheese, grated
⅔	cup half and half
½	teaspoon salt (optional)

Sauté onions in butter until limp but not brown. Combine with other ingredients and pour into a large casserole dish. Bake in a preheated 325 degree oven for about 45 minutes. Remove cover the last 15 minutes of baking time. This is especially good with any pork dish.

Serves 4 to 6.

Ms. Wright's Cheese Straws

1	pound sharp (block) Cheddar cheese
3	sticks butter
½	teaspoon red pepper flakes (adjust to taste)
	Dash of hot sauce
4	cups plain flour (approximately)

Allow cheese and butter to soften to room temperature. Grate cheese and mix thoroughly with butter using a wooden spoon. Add flour a little at a time until dough is stiff and no longer sticky; add red pepper flakes and hot sauce. A little more flour may be added if necessary. Fill cookie press using a star plate to form straws onto an un-greased cookie sheet. Bake at 350 degrees for about 8 to 10 minutes, but do not allow straws to brown. Remove from oven and place on baking rack to cool completely.

Ham Quiche
(From the kitchen of Margaret Debolt)

1 ½	cups grated Swiss cheese
¾	cup (or to taste) cooked ham, chopped
1	unbaked 9 inch deep dish, pie shell
3	eggs
¾	cup half and half
½	cup milk
½	teaspoon salt
¼	teaspoon pepper
⅛	teaspoon Cayenne pepper
½	teaspoon powdered mustard

Sprinkle cheese and ham in pie shell. Beat remaining ingredients and pour over cheese and ham. Bake in preheated 375 degree oven for 45 minutes. Cool on rack 15 minutes, and serve.

MARY HARTY'S ZUCCHINI CREAM SOUP

2	tablespoons green onions, finely chopped	2 ½	tablespoons butter
	1 clove garlic, minced	1	teaspoon curry powder
1	pound zucchini, cleaned, sliced thin	¼-½	teaspoon salt
		½	cup heavy cream
		1 ²/₃	cups chicken broth

In tightly covered pan simmer green onion, garlic and zucchini in the butter for about 8-10 minutes, until barley tender. Shake pan occasionally to prevent the vegetables from burning. Place mixture and remaining ingredients in blender or food processor until desired consistency. Serve either hot or cold. These freeze well, but if you freeze, omit the cream until time to serve. Garnish with bacon bits, sour cream and green onions.

GEORGIA BENNE SEED DRESSING
(From the kitchen of Margaret Debolt)

1	teaspoon paprika	1 or	2 cloves garlic, minced or crushed, to taste
½	teaspoon ground mustard		
½	teaspoon sugar	¾	cup peanut oil
½	teaspoon salt	4	teaspoons toasted benne
¼	cup white vinegar seed		Dash hot pepper sauce

Mix paprika, mustard, sugar, and salt well together, rubbing out any lumps. Stir in vinegar, hot pepper sauce, garlic, oil, and seed. Mix well and transfer to shaker container. Refrigerate until needed. Shake well before using.

Trivia: What makes Lucille Wright's tomato sandwiches enjoyable to eat? (#12)

MAGNOLIA WALDORF SALAD

1	cup apples, diced	¾	cup mayonnaise
1	cup celery, finely diced	½	cup raisins
	Salt and pepper to taste	½	cup walnuts or pecans, chopped

Combine all ingredients. Toss or stir then chill. Serve on bed of lettuce.

Fun Fact: Called sesame seeds today, the benne seed was first from Africa with the slave trade. It gives a distinctive flavor to Savannah cookies and candy.

CABBAGE ISLAND SALAD (COLESLAW)

1	head cabbage, medium	1	cup celery, diced
⅓	cup salad oil	1	green pepper, diced
1	tablespoon salt	½	teaspoon curry powder
¾	cup sugar	1	teaspoon oregano
1 ½	cups vinegar	1	teaspoon season all
1	medium onion, sliced	½	teaspoon garlic powder
2	carrots, grated		

Shred cabbage thin. In a saucepan combine salad oil, salt, sugar, and vinegar; bring to a boil. In a large bowl combine cabbage, onion, carrots, celery, and pepper; add spices and mix thoroughly. Pour hot salad oil mixture over cabbage, stirring in completely. This is a great summertime or anytime dish.

DAUGHTERS OF DESTINY

12 E. 41st Street
Savannah, Georgia 31401
(912) 663-0894

Daughters of Destiny is a spiritual women's center in Savannah, Georgia that holds weekly seminars to encourage all women, all ages, all denominations to stand up to their authentic selves and honor the truths that lie within. We are all links in the same chain, and as such are bound to each other through all the same joys, trials and tribulations. The group was founded by Miriam Center and has been ongoing for twenty years. Miriam began the group in Los Angeles and has held the same format across the country in various cities. The Daughters of Destiny Center was established in 2005 and encourages various women's outreach programs to be held at the center, a 1915 red cottage. Ms. Center also holds weekly seminars for recovering drug addicts at a drug rehabilitation center. Something magical takes place when women encourage one another on their inner and outer journeys to good health. Center says, "We are all links in the same chain, and who mothers the mothers of the world if not other women. We do it by instinct."

Fun Fact: Jim Williams was the one that gave Miriam Center her nickname in "The Book;" he called her 'Badness'. Miriam loved Mrs. Williams' caramel cake. Try it; I'm sure you will love it too!

SHRIMP WITH CASHEWS

CASHEWS MAKE THIS DISH: DON'T SUBSTITUTE

*(From the kitchen of Miriam Center
Daughters of Destiny, Savannah, Georgia)*

1	teaspoon cornstarch	4	tablespoons water
2	tablespoons sherry	½	teaspoon dark sesame oil
1	teaspoon sugar	½	teaspoon salt, or to taste
2	tablespoons corn, peanut or vegetable oil	1	pound raw shrimp, shelled and deveined
12	scallions (about 2 bunches) in 2-inch slices	1	cup cashews

In a bowl, mix the cornstarch and water together, stirring until dissolved. Stir in the sherry, sesame oil, sugar, and salt. Set aside. Heat the oil in a skillet over medium-high heat. Add the shrimp and scallions and sauté for about 2 minutes, stirring and tossing. Stir in the cashews and the cornstarch mixture; cook and continue stirring for about 1 minute, until slightly thickened.

VIDALIA ONION PIE
*(From the kitchen of Miriam Center
Daughters of Destiny, Savannah, Georgia)*

4	cups thinly sliced onions	1	cup crushed saltines
½	cup melted butter	4	slightly beaten eggs
1½	cups milk	1	cup Cheddar cheese

Melt ¼ cup butter and mix with saltines. Put in bottom of pie pan**. Sauté onions with remaining butter. Mix milk and eggs. Place onions in pie shell. Pour milk and egg mixture over onions. Add cheese to top. Bake 350 degrees for 30 minutes

** May use pyrex dish.

Trivia: With whom did the Adlers meet with in Washington, DC to discuss low-income housing? (#45)

LOU'S MEAT AND POTATO CASSEROLE

1½	pounds ground chuck	1	can cream of chicken soup
5	large white potatoes, sliced		Salt & pepper to taste or
4	large onions, sliced		Lady & Sons house
1	can cream of mushroom soup		seasoning*
	Mild or sharp Cheddar cheese		

In a saucepan brown meat, drain off fat. In a casserole dish, alternate layers of meat, potatoes, onions and seasoning. Mix soups together and pour over casserole. Cover and bake for 1 hour and 45 minutes at 375 degrees. Remove from oven and sprinkle the top with grated cheese. Return to oven for additional 15 minutes.

* The Lady & Sons house seasoning can be purchased from "The Book" Gift Shop.

MR. GLOVER'S HAMBURGER PIE

1	pound ground beef	1	medium (Vidalia) onion, chopped
2	teaspoons chili powder		
1	15 ½ ounce can tomatoes	1	15 ½ ounce can whole-kernel corn
1	15 ½ ounce can English peas		
1	15 ½ ounce can whole potatoes, diced	1	cup cornmeal
1	tablespoon baking powder	1	cup all-purpose flour
1 ½	cups buttermilk	1	egg, beaten
			Salt & Pepper to taste

Brown beef in skillet along with onion, salt, chili powder and a dash of Worcestershire sauce. Drain liquid from vegetables. Spread beef mixture in bottom of an oiled 3 quart baking dish; combine drained vegetables and spread over meat. Combine cornmeal, flour, salt, pepper and baking powder. Stir in beaten egg and buttermilk. Mix well and spoon over vegetable layer. Bake for 30-45 minutes or until brown at 400 degrees.

Trivia: What was the dice game that Jim Williams enjoyed playing? (#6)

NOUVEAU RICHE QUICHE LORRAINE

1	cup cream	4	egg yolks
	Pinch of salt, pepper, and nutmeg	1	package of bacon
¼	pound sharp Cheddar cheese, grated	¼	pound mild Cheddar cheese, grated

Blend together cream, egg yolks, salt, pepper and nutmeg. Set aside. Fry bacon until crisp and drain on paper towel. Fill prepared quiche shell or regular pie shell with overlapping layers of cheese and broken bacon. Pour blended mixture over cheese and bacon. Bake at 375 degrees for 35-45 minutes or until cheese is puffed and crust is brown.

SQUASH CASSEROLE
(The Pirates House)

3	cups yellow or zucchini squash, sliced	1	egg yolk, beaten
¼	cup sour cream or green onion tops	1	tablespoon chopped chives
2	tablespoons grated Cheddar cheese	¼	cup fresh bread crumbs
½	teaspoon salt	¼	cup grated Cheddar cheese
⅛	teaspoon paprika	3	tablespoons butter, melted
1	tablespoon butter or margarine		

Preheat oven to 350 degrees. Place squash in a small amount of water; cover pan. Bring to a boil, lower heat, and simmer until tender, about 6 to 8 minutes. Shake the pan to keep the squash from sticking (or use a steamer rack). Drain well. Combine sour cream, butter, grated cheese, salt and paprika. Remove from heat and stir in beaten egg yolk and chives or green onions. Add the squash and stir gently to mix. Place the mixture in a baking dish. Cover with bread crumbs mixed with ¼ cup cheese and 3 tablespoons butter. Bake for 20 minutes, or until top is brown. Let sit 5 minutes before serving.

Serves 4.

Trivia: How did Lady Astor describe Savannah? (#15)

GINGER'S CARROTS

3-4	cups sliced carrots	2	whole cloves
1	cup orange juice	¾	teaspoon ground ginger
½	cup chicken broth	1	teaspoon grated lime
3	tablespoons sugar		rind

Place all ingredients except sugar in saucepan and bring to a boil. Stir in sugar, cover and simmer for about 30 minutes or until carrots are just tender.

MR. GLOVER'S WALKING THE DOGS

1	can crescent rolls
4	hot dogs - favorite brand
	Silly salt*
	Wood sticks or skewers

Soak wood sticks in water for about 15 minutes while completing other process. Roll out 2 crescent rolls into a square; sprinkle with a little flour, a little silly salt and place hot dog on each square. Pinch edges together and press onto a wooden stick or skewer. Bake at 350 degrees or until golden brown. Serve with mustard for dipping.

Note: This is a great and fun project for the kids and also, a very tasty snack.

* Silly salt is a product of The Lady & Sons and may be purchased from "The Book" Gift Shop, (912) 233-3867.

Trivia: What city is Jim Williams originally from? (#74)

That Choose to Stay North of Gaston Street

MISS BLANCHE'S CARAMEL CAKE
(*From the kitchen of Miriam Center*)

	Butter
	Flour
3	large eggs
2	teaspoons pure vanilla extract
1	box plain white cake mix
8	ounces whole milk
	Caramel frosting (see below)
1	stick butter, melted

Preheat oven to 350 degrees placing rack in center. With butter, grease two 9-inch cake pans thoroughly, dust with flour, shake out excess; set aside.

In a large mixing bowl combine cake mix, milk, melted butter, eggs and vanilla. With an electric mixer blend at low speed for about 1 minute; scrap sides with spatula and mix for an additional two minutes at medium speed. After scraping down sides once again the batter should look well blended. Divide batter evenly into both pans, smoothing out with spatula.

Bake cakes until they are golden brown, about 25 to 30 minutes, or until cake springs back when lightly touched with finger. Remove from oven and cool on wire racks for 10 minutes. Run a knife along edge of each pan to insure cake does not stick, turn over, then turn back right side up; place on rack and allow to cool for an additional 30 minutes.

While cakes are cooling prepare Caramel Frosting (see next page).

Trivia: How many trials did Jim Williams go through? (#22)

CARAMEL FROSTING

1	stick butter	¼	cup whole milk
½	cup packed light brown sugar	2	cups confectioners' sugar, sifted
½	cup packed dark brown sugar	1 ¼	teaspoons pure vanilla extract

In a heavy saucepan combine butter and both brown sugars over medium heat; stir and bring to a boil, about 2 minutes. Add milk and bring back to a boil, stirring constantly. Remove from heat; add confectioners' sugar and vanilla. Beat with a wooden spoon until frosting is smooth.

Place one cake on serving platter. While frosting is still warm spread a layer over top of cake. Place second cake on top and continue frosting top and sides, quickly as frosting will set; if frosting starts to harden place back on stove at low heat for about 1 minute. Remove, and start frosting cake again. Once frosting has set on cake, cut and serve.

Note: You may freeze this cake for up to 6 months by wrapping in aluminum foil. Before serving remove from freezer and set out to thaw the night before.

Trivia: What had Jim purchased just before Jackie Onassis' visit? How much did it cost him? (#2)

(MILLS B.) LANE CAKE

(Inspired by The Pirates House)

2	sticks butter or margarine	2	teaspoons baking powder
2	cups sugar	1	cup milk
8	egg whites (keep yolks for filling, see below)	2	teaspoons vanilla extract
3 ¼	cups all-purpose flour, sifted		

Preheat oven to 375 degrees. Set out butter or margarine and egg whites to room temperature. Line the bottom of three 9-inch cake pans with wax paper. In a mixing bowl, cream butter and sugar until light and fluffy. Sift flour and baking powder together at least twice then add alternately with milk to creamed mixture, starting and ending with flour. Beat in vanilla. Beat egg whites until stiff but not dry and gently into creamed mixture; mix thoroughly. Divide mixture among the 3 pans; bake for 20 minutes or until golden brown and cake shrinks from sides of the pan. Cool on wire racks for at least 10 minutes, remove wax paper, then turn right side up to continue cooling.

FILLING

1	stick butter, softened	1	teaspoon vanilla extract
1	cup sugar	1	cup raisins
8	egg yolks (from above)	1	cup pecans, chopped
½	cup bourbon or brandy		(optional)

In a mixing bowl cream butter and sugar together. Beat in egg yolks. Place in a heavy pot over medium heat and cook, stirring constantly with a wooden spoon, until thick. Stir in bourbon or brandy, vanilla, raisins and nuts. Cool, spread between layers. Frost the entire cake with 7-minute icing (see recipe).

Refrigerate.

COCA-COLA® CAKE

1	package Betty Crocker® white cake mix	4	tablespoons unsweetened cocoa powder
1	stick butter or margarine	1	cup Coca-Cola®
½	cup buttermilk	2	large eggs, beaten
1	teaspoon vanilla extract		

Blend together all ingredients in a mixer for 1 minute on low speed. Scrape down and mix for another 2 minutes. Bake in a 350 degree preheated oven for about 40 minutes. Let cool for at least 15 minutes before applying icing.

(For our mid-west and northwest U.S. friends, you can call this Pop Cake).

ICING:

1	stick butter or margarine	4	tablespoons unsweetened cocoa powder
7	tablespoons Coca-Cola®		
1	teaspoon vanilla	1	box confectioners' sugar, sifted
1	cup toasted chopped pecans (optional)		

Place butter in saucepan over medium heat; stir in cocoa powder, cola and bring to a boil. Remove from heat and add sugar, vanilla and nuts (if used). Pour mixture and spread over cake.

Note: Savannah had one of the first Coca-Cola bottling plants. It once stood where the Mulberry Inn is located now on Washington Square. Part of structure is the original bottling factory.

You know you are getting old when
the candles cost more than the cake.

DRIGGER'S GRATED APPLE PIE

2	large apples, Granny Smith work well	1	egg
1	stick margarine	1	teaspoon cinnamon
2	tablespoons lemon juice	2 ¼	tablespoons flour

Peel apples and core. Grate apples and mix with other ingredients. Pour into a 9-inch unbaked pie shell and bake at 375 degrees for 45-60 minutes. (Place strips of aluminum foil around edge of crust if it gets too brown). Serve warm with vanilla ice cream and whipped cream.

NOGS MERRY SNOW MERINGUES

1	cup sugar		Parchment paper
4	egg whites	1	package M&M's® milk chocolate holiday candy

Preheat oven to 250 degrees. In a mixer combine sugar and egg whites; whip until frothy. Spoon mixture unto parchment-lined cookie sheets; sprinkle candies onto mounds and bake for about 1 hour or until bottoms are hard.

Note: Great decorating project for the kids during the holidays or anytime.

Never eat any product on which the listed ingredients cover more than one-third of the package.

Trivia: What did John Berendt dial to find an apartment? (#27)

SAVANNAH PEANUT BUTTER FUDGE
(From the kitchen of a Savannah NOG)

¼   cup butter or margarine
⅓   cup milk
⅔   cup chunky peanut butter
1   16 ounce package powdered sugar
½   cup cocoa
¼   teaspoon salt
1   teaspoon vanilla extract

In a medium saucepan melt butter or margarine; remove from heat and add milk and vanilla. Sift powdered sugar, cocoa and salt together; gradually add powdered sugar mixture to milk mixture, stirring until well blended. Stir in chunky peanut butter and press into a battered 8-inch square pan. Cover and chill; cut into squares.

Yields about 2 dozen.

MARY HARTY'S DIVINITY

3   cups sugar
¾   cup light corn syrup
½   cup water
3   egg whites

1   teaspoon vanilla extract
1   cup pecans, finely
    chopped
    Pinch of salt

In a large saucepan combine sugar, corn syrup, water and salt. Cook over high heat until mixture becomes hardened; on a candy thermometer temperature should be about 265 degrees. Beat egg whites until stiff, add salt. Carefully and slowly pour syrup into egg whites beating until rich and creamy. Beat in vanilla and pecans. While mixture is still hot, carefully drop by spoonfuls onto wax paper and let cool. Be creative and add your favorite food coloring while beating in syrup.

9 DIME TEA COOKIES

3   eggs
1   cup oil
4   teaspoons vanilla flavoring
1   teaspoon lemon flavoring
½   cup sugar
4   cups self-rising flour, sifted
     Pecans or walnuts

In a mixing bowl beat eggs; stir in oil, vanilla and lemon. Add sugar, blending together well. Add flour and nuts and mix until blended.

Drop by spoonfuls onto an un-greased cookie sheet. Bake at 400 degrees until bottoms are golden brown. Every oven will be a little different; check after 8 to 10 minutes.

Trivia: What is the epitaph on John Herndon Mercer's grave? (#10)

OLD-FASHIONED BENNE CANDY
(From the kitchen of Margaret Debolt)

1   pound light brown sugar
2   tablespoons butter
½   cup milk
1   tablespoon cider vinegar
1 ½ cups toasted benne seeds
1   teaspoon vanilla extract

Combine first four ingredients in a large, heavy saucepan and bring to a boil. Continue to cook until soft ball stage or 236 degrees on the candy thermometer, stirring very little. Take off the stove and cool until bottom of pan is comfortably warm on palm of hand, or to 110 degrees on the candy thermometer. Beat in benne seeds. Add vanilla and beat until creamy and slightly thick. Drop by teaspoonfuls onto a buttered dish or paper, and let stand until firm. Store the candy in an airtight container in a cool place.

TAGLIOLI'S BREAD PUDDING
(In honor of Jimmy Taglioli)

2	cups milk	2	teaspoons vanilla extract
2	cups sugar, granulated	3	cups cubed stale bread *
5	large eggs, beaten		(if no stale bread, cut fresh
1	cup chopped pecans		and leave out overnight)
1 ¼	cups packed light brown sugar		
½	stick butter, softened		

Preheat oven to 350 degrees. Set stale bread into a bowl. In another bowl mix sugar, eggs and milk; add vanilla. Pour mixture over bread and let sit while making up rest of recipe. In a bowl mix brown sugar and butter; add pecans. In a greased 13x9x2-inch pan, pour in bread mixture. Let sit for 5 minutes then sprinkle other mixture over top and bake for 40 to 45 minutes. Remove from oven and add topping sauce (see below).

* Great idea for stale bread. No reason to throw it away. Make this up for your friends and family as a present (instead of fruitcake).

TOPPING SAUCE

1	cup sugar	2 ½	teaspoons vanilla extract
1	stick melted butter	⅓	cup brandy (or a little
1	egg, beaten		more to taste)

In a saucepan, mix together sugar, butter, egg and vanilla over medium heat until sugar is melted. Remove from heat; add brandy stirring in well. Pour mixture over bread pudding.

Great served warm or cold.

Trivia: How did Mary Harty describe the squares? (#57)

SAVANNAH FLOATING ISLAND
(From the kitchen Margaret Debolt and Emma R. Law)
A very old and favorite recipe

CUSTARD:

3	egg yolks, beaten	2	cups milk, scalded
¼	cup sugar	½	teaspoon vanilla or
¼	teaspoon salt		almond extract

Make Custard: Mix egg yolks, sugar, and salt in top of double boiler. Slowly stir in milk. Cool over hot (not boiling) water, stirring constantly, until mixture coats a metal spoon, about 6 to 8 minutes. Remove from heat. Strain, if desired, in case bits of egg whites have clung to the egg yolks. Stir in extract, and chill in a shallow float bowl.

MERINGUE:

Make Meringue: beat egg whites until stiff but not dry. Beat in salt. Add sugar, very gradually, beating all the while. Drop by heaping teaspoons into boiling water. Meringue should be "set" in 2 to 3 minutes. Lift gently on slotted spoon, drain a bit, and place on top of custard. Finish Meringues, place on top of custard, and let stand in a cool place until time to serve.

Trivia: What role did Jimmy Talioli play in Jim Williams's life? (#83)

BRANDIED GRAPES
(From the kitchen of Margaret Debolt)

1	teaspoon lemon juice	2 ½	cups halved seedless
¼	cup honey		grapes
2	tablespoons brandy		Commercial sour cream
	Grated nutmeg		

Combine juice, honey, and brandy. Add grapes and marinate well, covered, in the refrigerator for at least three hours; overnight is even better. Serve in sherbet cups with a dollop of sour cream and a whisper of grated nutmeg on the cream.

NOGS GRASSHOPPER FREEZE

1 ¼	cups finely crushed Vanilla Wafers	3	well-beaten egg yolks
3 - 4	tablespoons butter, melted	1 ½	cups sifted confectioners' sugar
1	quart peppermint ice cream, softened	½	cup chopped pecans (we call them pee cans down here)
2	squares unsweetened chocolate	1	teaspoon vanilla
3	egg whites		

Mix wafer crumbs with melted butter. Reserve ¼ cup crumb mixture for topping. Press remaining crumb mixture into 9x9x2 inch baking pan. Spread with ice cream and freeze. Melt ½ cup butter and chocolate over low heat; gradually stir into egg yolks with confectioners' sugar, nuts and vanilla. Cool thoroughly. Beat egg whites until stiff peaks form. Beat chocolate mixture until smooth; fold in egg whites. Spread chocolate mixture over ice cream; top with reserved crumb mix; freeze. May be served with favorite chocolate sauce or hot fudge sauce.

MARY HARTY'S BLACK BOTTOM PIE

1	9 inch graham cracker crumb crust	3	egg whites
1	tablespoon gelatin	¼	teaspoon salt
¼	cup cold water	¼	teaspoon cream of tartar
½	cup sugar	2	cups milk
2	tablespoons powdered sugar	3 ½	teaspoons cornstarch
1 ½	ounces melted semisweet chocolate	4	egg yolks
	Chocolate curls to garnish	½	teaspoon vanilla
		1 ¼	tablespoons rum

Soak gelatin in water and set aside. Beat the egg yolks until light. Scald the milk and stir slowly into egg yolks. Add the sugar and cornstarch into the mixture. Cook this mixture over hot water, stirring constantly, for about 20 minutes or until the custard will coat a spoon. Take out 1 cupful of the custard and add it to the melted chocolate, beating until well-blended and cool. Add the vanilla and pour this custard into the pie shell. Dissolve the soaked gelatin into remaining custard; custard needs to be hot enough to melt gelatin. Let it cool, but do not let it stiffen. When cool, add the rum. Beat the egg whites, salt and cream of tartar until very stiff, adding the sugar gradually, a teaspoon at a time. Fold the egg whites into the custard. Cover the chocolate custard with the rum-flavored custard. Chill until the pie sets. Whip the cream, gradually adding the powdered sugar. Cover the custard with the whipped cream and cover the top with chocolate curls (run a vegetable peeler over the side of a solid candy bar).

Trivia: What did Mary Harty pack for the excursion to Bonaventure Cemetery? (#35)

UGA V'S BULLDOG BITES!

(From the kitchen of Mr. & Mrs. Sonny Seiler
Owner of the Uga, Mascot for the University of Georgia)

Uga is very fond of cheese! He enjoys this treat as an appetizer before eating his Hill's dog food.

1	pound sausage (hot or mild)
2	cups sharp grated cheese
3	cups Bisquick
1	teaspoon Worcestershire sauce
2	drops Tabasco sauce (optional)

Mix together all ingredients thoroughly. Shape dough into small balls. Bake on cookie sheet at 350 degrees for 20 minutes. May be frozen and reheated. Also, travels well to football games.

Note: This is an exceptional idea for a tailgate party or football party at home.

Uga V

Trivia: Who was Jim Williams' primary lawyer? (#32)

PATRICK'S DOGGIE BISCUITS

2 ½	cups whole wheat flour	1	teaspoon beef bouillon
½	cup ice water		(granules)
½	cup powered milk	6	tablespoons bacon
1	teaspoon garlic powder		grease or meat drippings
1	tablespoon wheat germ	1	egg

In a mixing bowl combine flour, powered milk, garlic powder, wheat germ, and bouillon. Stir in drippings; add egg and enough ice water for mixture to form a ball. Pat out to about ½-inch thick; cut desired length and shape. Bake in a preheated oven of 350 degrees for 25-30 minutes. Cool.

Note: These are really Dog Biscuits so <u>do not </u>feed to your husband or children, unless you want to go out to dinner, then tell them this is all they get. Enjoy.

Trivia: Mr. Glover would walk Patrick the dog. Who was Patrick's owner? (#91)

MARRIED WOMEN'S CARD CLUB

The Gingerbread House © 1996 Sharon Saseen

These are a compilation of recipes from the
Book and Card Club, and yes, they still meet today.

FABERGE EGGS

6	hard boiled eggs	1	teaspoon sweet relish
1	tablespoon mayonnaise (add more if yolks are large)	1	teaspoon yellow mustard Paprika, to garnish

Cut eggs in halves and remove yolks. Mash yolks with fork. Mix with the above ingredients; salt and pepper to taste. Stuff eggs and refrigerate. You can also use a pastry tip in a plastic baggie; stuff ingredients inside after mashing up, then squeeze into egg halves. Sprinkle with paprika to garnish.

MWC CLUB LAYERED CHEESE SQUARES

½	pound sharp Cheddar cheese, grated	1	egg
½	pound butter, softened	¼	teaspoon paprika
		3	slices white bread, thin-sliced

Place together 3 slices of thin-sliced white bread, trim crusts and cut into quarters; making 4 stacks of 3 layers. Spread top of each slice, sides and bottom of the stack with the above mixture.
Place on baking sheet and bake in oven at 350 degrees for about 20 minutes or until cheese is melted and squares are lightly brown. These freeze well and can be prepared for later baking. Freeze on cookie sheet; then place in bags for storage.

Trivia: When and why was the Married Women's Card Cub started? (#8)

Savannah Seafood Quiche
(Shrimp, Crab or Lobster)

1	small onion, minced
2	tablespoons margarine or butter
1	cup cooked crab, shrimp or lobster (cut up)
	Dash salt & pepper
¼	cup dry white wine
3	eggs
1	cup half and half
1	tablespoon tomato paste
1	8 inch partially cooked pastry shell
¼	cup Swiss cheese, grated

Sauté onion in margarine or butter until soft, add seafood and stir 2-3 minutes. Add wine, salt and pepper. Set aside. Beat eggs; add cream, tomato paste and seasonings. Add seafood and pour into pastry shell. Sprinkle with cheese and bake in oven at 350 to 375 degrees for about 30 minutes or until set.

Trivia: What color did Serena Dawes wrap herself up in to attend Jim Williams' Christmas party? (#46)

Pamela Lee

MICROWAVE FLOUNDER
(From the kitchen of Margaret Debolt)

1	pound flounder or other fillets
2	tablespoons butter or margarine, melted (not diet type)
1	teaspoon fresh lemon juice
2	tablespoons dry white wine or white grape juice
3	green onions, finely chopped
½	cup raw mushrooms, sliced
1	large tomato, peeled, seeded and cubed
½	teaspoon salt

Arrange fillets in a large microwave baking dish with thick edges toward the outside. Stir together remaining ingredients and spread over fish. Cover with waxed paper and cook on High for 5 minutes. Let stand a few minutes before serving.

Note: For two, you can use less fish, but still keep the same amount of other ingredients, and adjust time accordingly.

To peel tomatoes, (if you want to), drop in boiling water and let stand a few minutes; skin comes right off. This is a very nutritious dish.

Serves 4.

LUCILLE WRIGHT

Although Ms. Lucille is no longer with us, a sweet memory of bygone days still linger in the hearts of native Savannahians. In her day she was the most sought-after caterer in Savannah. Her food was in such high demand that parties were sometimes rescheduled to suit her availability. Jim Williams loved to entertain and quite lavishly. His Christmas party was the highlight of Savannah's social season, and it would not be complete without the delectable bites of Ms. Lucille. "The Book" *Midnight in the Garden of Good and Evil* will introduce you to Mrs. Wright on page 8.

LUCILLE WRIGHT'S TOMATO SANDWICHES

BREAD:

Use thin slices, whole wheat on the bottom, white on the top. Cut the bread into circles with a biscuit cutter, and remove the circle of bread. Prepare the bread a day ahead, if you like.

SPREAD:

Mix a little grated onion (too much makes it bitter), black pepper, and Accent into Hellmann's mayonnaise. No measurements here. Make it to taste. Spread the bread a day ahead. Cover and refrigerate.

TOMATOES:

Peel, slice, and drain thoroughly between layers of paper towels. (Soggy tomatoes make soggy sandwiches.) Sprinkle the tomatoes with Lawry's Seasoned Salt before assembling the sandwiches. You may prepare the sandwiches several hours before a party. Cover with a damp tea towel and refrigerate.

> *Trivia: What makes Lucille Wright's tomato sandwiches enjoyable to eat? (#12)*

LUCILLE WRIGHT'S OYSTER BISQUE

1   quart oysters (extra pint optional)
Freshly grated nutmeg
Curry powder
Accent
1   medium onion, chopped
1   tablespoon Worcestershire sauce
2   cups heavy cream
4   tablespoons butter
     Chopped fresh parsley

4   tablespoons all-purpose flour
     Salt and black pepper
4   stalks celery, cut into medium size pieces
1   tablespoon fresh lemon juice
4   cups milk
     Cayenne pepper
     Paprika

Pick over the oysters for shells. Simmer the oysters in a covered pot over low heat with a little salt and black pepper. Stir occasionally until the edges of the oysters curl. Lift the oysters out of the stock with a slotted spoon and put them in a colander with a bowl underneath to catch the pot liquor. Pour the stock from the pot into the bowl, being careful to discard any oyster dregs. Set the stock aside.

Cook the celery and onion in a little water until tender; drain, reserving the broth. Add the broth to the oyster stock (should measure about 2 cups), then add the milk and cream (reserve a little cream to whip for garnish).

Heat the butter, then whisk in the flour to make a roux. Add the stock mixture to the roux, and stir briskly until thickened and smooth. Add a little nutmeg, a pinch of curry powder, a pinch of Accent, the lemon juice, Worcestershire, and cayenne. Correct the seasonings. Mash the oysters with the celery and onions and mix well; add to oyster stock. Keep warm over hot water until time to serve. Whip the reserved cream. Pour bisque into individual bowls. Swirl an even portion of whipped cream into each bowl. Add a little paprika and chopped parsley to garnish. Offer sherry separately, if desired.

Yields 2 ½ Quarts.

MWCC Tomato Pie

1   deep dish pie crust
4-6 large, ripe tomatoes, sliced and dried between
      paper towels
1   onion, sliced into rings
      Italian seasoning to taste
      Salt and pepper to taste
1 ½ cups grated Mozzarella cheese
1 ½ cups mayonnaise (we use Hellmann's)

Bake pie crust for 5 to 10 minutes at 400 degrees. Layer sliced tomatoes, onion, Italian seasoning, salt and pepper, and ½ cup of cheese. Mix remaining cheese and mayonnaise together and repeat with second layer. Bake for 30 to 40 minutes at 350 degrees or until pie browns.

Peanut Soup

(From the kitchen of Margaret Debolt and
Georgia Peanut Committee)

¼   cup butter
1   cup thinly sliced celery
1   medium onion, chopped fine
2   tablespoons flour
2   quarts chicken stock or broth
1   cup creamy peanut butter
1   cup light cream

Melt butter in large saucepan over low heat; add celery and onion. Cook until tender, but not browned. Add flour and stir until mixture is smooth. Gradually add chicken broth and bring to a boil. Blend in peanut butter and simmer about 15 minutes. Stir in cream just before serving.

WASTE NOT

You ought not to waste fat of any description, or anything else that may be turned to account; such as marrow-bones, or any other clean bones from which food may be extracted in the way of soup, broth, or stock…. Remember, "Wilful waste makes moeful want."

THE GUIDE TO SERVICE, 1842

GEORGIA NUGGETS

(From the kitchen of Margaret Debolt)

3	cups light brown sugar, firmly packed	½	teaspoon vanilla extract
⅛	teaspoon salt	1 ½	tablespoons butter or margarine
1	cup light cream	2	cups coarsely chopped pecans

Dissolve sugar and salt in cream in a 4-quart saucepan. Cook over moderate heat, stirring occasionally, until mixture reaches soft ball stage or 236 degrees on candy thermometer. Remove from heat and cool on rack until bottom of pan is comfortably warm on palm of hand, or 110 degrees on candy thermometer. Add vanilla, butter, and pecans. Beat until mixture is creamy and thick. Drop by tablespoons onto heavy waxed paper. When "set" and cool, store in air-tight container in a cool place.

Trivia: How many women are allowed in the Married Women's Card Club at any one time? What important criteria must one meet to be a part of this club? (#7)

MWCC LADY FINGERS

2   sticks butter
2   cups plain all-purpose finely ground   flour
1   cup pecans,
1   teaspoon vanilla
½   cup confectioners' sugar
1   teaspoon vanilla butter-nut flavoring
¼   teaspoon salt
2   teaspoons water

Preheat oven to 325 degrees. In a mixing bowl cream butter; add pecans, vanilla, vanilla butter-nut and water. Add in flour, sugar and salt. Shape into balls; then form into finger-like cookies. Place onto cookie sheet and bake until lightly browned on bottom. After cookies have cooled roll in confectioner's sugar. Serve immediately or put up in container; these will keep for some time.

Note: These are great for Card Club or Book Club and are pretty too.

Fun Fact: Did you know how long it had been since Jim Williams had his **last** Christmas Party? 8 years.

TREASURE ISLAND RUM TORTE
(From the kitchen of a Savannah NOG)

½	cup butter
1 ⅓	cups sugar
4	egg yolks, large
1	4 ounce Cool Whip
1	teaspoon instant coffee
1 ¼	teaspoons vanilla
16	ladyfingers
½	cup rum
¼	cup liquid strong coffee

Dissolve instant coffee in liquid strong coffee for 'Pirate' strength; set aside to cool. Cream butter, gradually adding sugar, and beat until fluffy; beat in egg yolks one at a time. Continue beating until very creamy; about 5 minutes. Stir in cooled coffee. Line a 9¼ x 5¼ x 2¾-inch loaf pan with wax paper. Place a layer of halved ladyfingers to cover bottom of pan. Pour about a quarter of rum. Spread about a third of the cream mixture over the ladyfingers. Repeat this process so that you have 4 layers of ladyfingers and 3 layers of the creamed mixture, beginning and ending with ladyfingers. Chill in refrigerator overnight. When ready to serve, place onto platter and frost with Cool Whip, flavored with rum and vanilla. Decorate with cherries, if desired. Slice thin to serve up to 10.

MWCC FRESH APPLE CAKE
(From the kitchen of Martha Giddens Nesbit)

1 ½	cups vegetable oil
2	cups sugar
3	eggs
3	cups flour
1	teaspoon salt
1	teaspoon baking soda
2	teaspoons vanilla
3	freshly chopped apples
1	cup chopped pecans

FILLING:

½	cup butter
¼	cup evaporated milk
1	cup light brown sugar
1	teaspoon vanilla extract

With electric mixer, combine oil and sugar until light and fluffy. Add slightly beaten eggs. Beat well. Sift together flour, salt, and soda. Add flour mixture to oil mixture. Batter will be very thick. Add vanilla, chopped apples and pecans. Mix well by hand.

Pour batter into 11x15 inch baking pan. Bake at 350 degrees for 30 minutes. Cool. Split cake in half. Pour filling over bottom layer, then top with second layer. Pour filling over top. Filling will run down sides, so you may keep spooning back over top and sides.

For filling, boil butter, milk and brown sugar over medium heat for 5 minutes. Add vanilla. Pour warm over layers.

For moister cake, make double recipe of filling. Cake is best made one day in advance so filling can seep into cake. Serves 10 to 12.

MINT JULEPS
(From the home bar of Martha Giddens Nesbit)

Mint syrup Crushed ice
Kentucky bourbon
Mint sprigs for garnish

MINT SYRUP

1   cup sugar
2   cups lightly packed
    fresh mint
1   cup water

Combine sugar and water in saucepan. Bring to a boil, stirring gently to dissolve; then boil 5 minutes without stirring. Remove from heat, add mint and cover saucepan; let sit until cool. Strain into jar. Keep refrigerated. Makes about 1 ½ cups.

For each drink, fill tall glass with crushed ice. Add 1 jigger mint syrup and 1 ½ jiggers of bourbon. Stir. Add more ice if necessary. Garnish with sprig of mint.

Trivia: When and why was the Married Women's Card Cub started? (#8)

"THE SENTIMENTAL GENTLEMAN"

Hamilton Turner Mansion © Sharon Saseen

JOE ODOM'S
ST. PADDY'S DAY
MENU AND MORE

Joe Odom's St. Paddy's Day
Corned Beef and Cabbage

1	3 pound corned beef brisket	1	teaspoon salt
1	large head green cabbage	1	teaspoon pepper
6	tablespoons butter	¼	teaspoon garlic

In a large stock pot, place corned beef; fill pot to nearly full with cold water and cover. Bring to a boil, reduce heat and simmer for about 3 hours or until corned beef is tender. Remove from pot. Chop up cabbage, place in colander and rinse leaves in cool water. In a separate pot melt butter and add cabbage leaving water on the leaves. Stir and cook until cabbage is well coated with butter. Sprinkle with salt, pepper and garlic. Cover pot and simmer until the cabbage is tender but still a little crisp, about 7 to 10 minutes.

Slice corned beef thinly. Place cabbage on plate and place beef on top. Sprinkle a spoonful or two of stock on top of corned beef and cabbage if it appears to be dry. Can be eaten just as is, but traditionally we serve it with mash potatoes.

Trivia: What three rules did Joe Odom tell John Berendt he should follow in order to fit in? What rule did he break? (#52)

Gloria's Corned Beef & Cabbage

2	pounds corned beef	2	tablespoons butter
½	cabbage, washed, cored and quartered		

Remove brine from corned beef, place in pot; cover with water and bring to boil over low heat. When water has boiled for 10 minutes, scrape off foam, cover pot and simmer until meat is tender; about 2 or 2 ½ hours. Remove beef, add cabbage to water with butter then replace beef on top of cabbage. Cook 5 minutes on low after bringing to a boil. Serves 4.

JOE'S IRISH STEW

2	pounds lean boneless stew beef		
1	medium onion, chopped	½	cup celery
4	medium-sized carrots, sliced	4	potatoes, peeled and cut
1	can tomatoes and juice		into small pieces
1	8 ounce can tomato sauce	1	can cut green beans
1	tablespoon sugar		and juice
2 ¼	cups water		Salt & pepper to taste

Flour stew beef and brown in a small amount of oil in stock pot with lid. Add water and cook on low heat for 1 hour. Add other ingredients and bring to a boil. Turn heat to low and cook for approximately 2 hours. (If you are anything like Joe; have an adult beverage with this stew).

Note: If you've never experienced a St. Patrick's Day in Savannah, you need to come one year, but plan early as hotels fill up quickly. Those that have read "The Book" should know that this was one of Joe's favorite times of the year.

Trivia: Gloria would sing a few lines from what song for the guests at the Hamilton-Turner House? (#58)

JOE'S SQUATTER FRITTERS

3-4	yellow squash	1	medium onion, diced
½	cup cracker crumbs		Salt & pepper to taste
2	eggs, beaten Vegetable oil		

Cook squash, drain and mash. In a large bowl combine squash, cracker crumbs, eggs, onion, salt and pepper. In a heavy saucepan pour vegetable oil, about 2-inches deep and heat to 375 degrees. Carefully drop mixture by the spoonful into hot oil until golden brown on both sides. Remove onto paper towels to dry. Great appetizer to serve warm. Makes about 10 fritters.

JOE'S ST. PADDY'S DAY SHRIMP AND GREEN NOODLE CASSEROLE

3-3½ pounds raw shrimp
4¼ tablespoons melted butter
5 green onions
1 cup mayonnaise
Dash of pepper
1 6 ounce package green noodles
Parmesan cheese
Pinch of salt
Paprika

1 cup sour cream
1½ teaspoon Dijon mustard
3 teaspoons vermouth or sherry
6 ounce grated Cheddar cheese
1 can cream of mushroom soup

Peel and devein raw shrimp; sauté in butter until just pink, being careful not to overcook (overcooking shrimp will make them tough). Refrigerate shrimp until ready to mix into casserole. Cook the green noodles as per instructions on package; drain and toss with 2 tablespoons of butter; sauté onion in remaining butter. Mix all other ingredients. (Now, if you're like Joe you would not use a measuring spoon for his vermouth or sherry. This was always added according to his taste, which is usually strong). Place buttered noodles in casserole, cover with shrimp and green onions. Pour other mixture on top and adjust, again, for seasoning taste (add more vermouth or sherry). Sprinkle with paprika and Parmesan cheese and bake for 30-35 minutes at 350 degrees. (After cooling, taste one last time to see if more vermouth or sherry is needed; not really). Enjoy!!

Trivia: What was Joe Odom doing when John Berendt first encountered him? (#44)

EYES OF MARCH BEER SOUP

1 quart chicken broth	1 teaspoon pepper
2-2 ½ pounds potatoes, chopped	¾ pound Cheddar cheese,
1 small onion, chopped	shredded
1 quart 2% milk	1 cup beer
3 ½-4 tablespoons soy sauce	Paprika to garnish

In a large pot pour in chicken broth and bring to a boil; add potatoes and onions. Simmer for 30 minutes, stirring occasionally. Remove from heat, allow soup to cool down; add milk. A little at a time, puree this mixture in a food processor then return to pot. Add soy sauce and pepper and stir well. Slowly bring soup back to simmer; add cheese, stirring well. Once cheese melts, add beer, stir, put into serving bowl, garnish with paprika. Serves 6.

Note: Some would add green food coloring if serving this soup on St. Paddy's Day. Remember, everything is green and everyone is Irish on March 17th in Savannah.

Trivia: Joe was proprietor, president and featured performer of a three-man jazz combo at what piano bar? (#70)

DAWE'S GREEN BOA SALAD

2 small packages instant pistachio pudding (sugar-free may be used)
1 can crushed pineapple, drained
1 small tub Cool Whip (light Cool Whip may be used)
½ bag mini marshmallows
1 jar drained cherries, cut in half
   Walnuts can be added if desired as garnishment or garnish top with some chopped pistachios

Mix instant pudding as per instructions on package. Add in other ingredients and pour into decorative bowl; refrigerate. Garnish when ready to serve. Very easy, very tasty, kids love it.

Whipped Leprechauns

(From the kitchen of Martha Gibbens Nesbit)

1	package chocolate wafers, crushed	½	gallon vanilla ice cream
½	cup crème de menthe (for garnish)	½	cup crème de menthe
	Mint leaves or chocolate mint candy	1	cup heavy cream, whipped

Thaw ice cream until soft. Mix ½ cup crème de menthe with ice cream; alternate layers of crushed wafers and ice cream in parfait glasses. Freeze before serving, top with dollop of whipped cream and pour slight amount of crème de menthe over whipped cream. Garnish with mint leaves or chocolate mint candy.

Makes 8 parfaits.

Trivia: What is Serena Dawes real name? (#20)

Sweet Georgia Brownies

4	eggs, beaten lightly	¼	teaspoon salt
2	cups sugar	⅓	cup cocoa powder
¾	cups butter, melted	4	Snicker candy bars, finely chopped
2	teaspoons vanilla extract		
1 ½	cups all-purpose flour	3	Hershey candy bars with almonds, finely chopped
½	teaspoon baking powder		

In a large bowl combine eggs, sugar, butter, and vanilla extract. In another bowl combine flour, baking powder, salt and cocoa powder; stir into sugar mixture. Stir in chopped snickers.

Spoon batter into a greased and floured 13x9x2-inch pan; sprinkle chopped Hershey candy bars over top. Bake for 30 to 35 minutes at 350 degrees. Cool on wire rack, and then cut into squares.

Yields abut 2 ½ dozen.

MANDY'S CHERRY PIE CAKE

1	can cherry pie filling (any pie filling will do)	1	cup chopped nuts
½	box yellow cake mix	½	stick butter

Put pie filling in an 8-inch square purex dish. Cover with cake mix and bake 30 minutes at 350 degrees. Add nuts and melted butter on top and bake an additional 20 minutes. Cut into squares and serve.

Note: Since you are only using half the mix why not use other half and make another pie for your neighbor.

MANDY'S BLONDIES

3	eggs	1	stick margarine, melted
1	box light brown sugar	2	cups self-rising flour
	Nuts (optional)		

In a mixing bowl beat eggs; add margarine then sugar. Blend together well with mixer. Slowly add flour making sure all mixes well. Add nuts, if desired. Pour into greased 9x13x2 inch pan and bake at 350 degrees for 30 to 35 minutes.

GLORIA'S 1, 2, 3, 4 CAKE

1	cup shortening	1	teaspoon vanilla
2	cups sugar	1	cup milk
3	cups flour*	4	eggs

Beat sugar and shortening together until creamy. Add eggs, one at a time, mixing in well. Beat in vanilla; add both flour and milk alternating between each. Pour mixture into bundt pan and bake at 350 degrees for about 1 hour. If using 8-inch pans, you should be able to fill 3; bake at 350 degrees for 30 minutes.

* 1 cup self-rising flour, 2 cups all-purpose flour

Trivia: In how many houses did Joe Odom live? (#18)

IRISH COFFEE

FOR EACH CUP:
½ to 1 ounce Irish whiskey   1-2 teaspoons sugar
½ to ¾ strong black coffee, hot   Lemon and sugar
2 tablespoons lightly whipped cream

Rub lemon slice around rim of glass mug. Dip in sugar to coat rim of glass. Pour in coffee. Add sugar and stir. Add whiskey. Slide whipped cream off of spoon so that it floats on top of coffee.

BALL AND CHAIN MARTINI

2 shots berry-flavored vodka
1 shot orange liqueur
Splash of lime juice
Blueberries to garnish, fresh or frozen (thawed)

In an ice-filled cocktail shaker, add vodka, liqueur and lime juice.
Shake; pour into martini glass through strainer. Garnish with blueberries.
Note: We use the tall "Birdgirl" shot glass which is actually about 1½ shots. You may purchase these from "The Book" Gift Shop, (912) 233-3867.

Trivia: Joe Odom would have been married how many times if he had taken Mandy as his wife? (#3)

"THE BOOK"
GIFT SHOP

Mercer House © Sharon Saseen

FAMILY AND FRIENDS

"THE BOOK" GIFT SHOP

127 East Calhoun Square
Savannah, Georgia 31401
(912) 233-3867
(888) 833-3867 for orders
Web:www.midnightinsavannah.com
Email: birdgirl10@prodigy.net

This is where an idea first began; to center a shop based on a best-selling book by John Berendt, a Yankee magazine writer, entitled *Midnight in the Garden of Good and Evil*," a book about Savannah with characters from in and around Savannah. It involves ladies who compared notes on their husband's suicides, to black drag queens and even a voodoo priestess who works her roots at midnight. The center of attention however focuses on an antique dealer, Jim Williams, and the crime he did or did not commit. It is truly a very good story and well written. If you do not already own "The Book" pick up your copy from "The Book" Gift Shop and add it to your family library.

Deborah Sullivan not only ran with the idea of centering her shop around "The Book," she allowed her creative juices to flow and soon the flood gates opened. She transformed an old dentist office and former real estate office into a 5-room 'mini museum'. Throughout her shop you will find a variety of items focusing on "The Book". Deborah ran with an idea with the blessing of John Berendt, and Jack Leigh, the photographer who captured the much talked about "Birdgirl" statue, as it once stood in eternal peace. With permission from Jack and from the Judson and Haynes families, Deborah was able to create various tributes honoring the "Bird Girl," the former centerpiece of the Trosdal Family (Garden) cemetery plot.

Today, her mini-museum is still a center of attraction for tourist from all around the world. Those coming to 'The Shop' are often amazed at how many items are centered around "The Book". It is truly an amazing site to come and see. We hope that everyone interested in our historic city with its wealth of stories and tall tales as part of its lore, will come to Savannah and visit with us.

Trivia: More than anyone else, this Georgia landscape architect suggested John Berendt write this book. Can you name him? (acknowledgement section)

CHEESE CRISPS
(From the kitchen of Deborah Sullivan)

2	cups all-purpose flour
1	teaspoon salt
1	cup pecans, chopped finely
2	cups grated sharp Cheddar cheese
1	tablespoon sugar
2	sticks margarine

Combine flour, sugar, and salt. Cut in margarine until mixture is crumbly. Add cheese and blend. Stir in pecans. Shape dough into 2 rolls 1 ½ inches in diameter. Wrap roll in waxed paper. Chill; cut 1/8-inch thick slices, place on non-greased cookie sheet and bake at 350 degrees for 10 to 15 minutes. Remove immediately to keep from crumbling.

BEEF AND BEAN DIP
(From the kitchen of our good friends Ron & Kay Walker)

2	pounds ground beef
2	large onions, chopped
2	pounds shredded Velveeta
1	cup ketchup
1	small jar green olives, save some juice
1	small jar black olives, save all juice
2	cans kidney beans (mashed and some juice)

Brown meat with 2/3 of the onions until it crumbles. Add ketchup and kidney beans. Cook about 20 minutes. Pour into 9x13x2-inch pan; top with cheese, onions and olives. Bake at 350 degrees for 30 minutes.

Note: Great with crackers, potato skins or large chips.

A good wife laughs at her husband's jokes, not because they are clever, but because she is.

DEB'S SESAME CHEESE BISCUITS
(From the kitchen of Deborah Sullivan)

Remove 1 roll of biscuits from your refrigerator and cut each in half. Roll into crescents and roll each into melted butter, Parmesan cheese or sesame seeds. Bake until brown, according to package.

Note: These can be two diffrent recipes; one with Parmesan cheese and the second with sesame seeds.

GRANNY D'S SWEET ROLL
(From the kitchen of Deb's grandmother, Florence Dimick)

2	cups milk, scalded	3	eggs, beaten
2	packages yeast	5	cups flour
¼	cup lukewarm water		
1	cup shortening (Crisco)		

Scald milk; cool to lukewarm. In another bowl stir yeast with lukewarm water; add shortening, set aside. Stir in sugar to milk, add beaten eggs; pour into yeast mixture. Mix in flour and let rise until doubled; knead down, then let it rise again. Make into rolls and bake at 370 degrees for 12 to 15 minutes or until lightly browned.

HOT ROLLS
(From the kitchen of Charlotte Dimick's Mother
Hazel Girrard)

1	package yeast	1	cup warm water
¼	cup warm water	½	cup oil
½	cup sugar	1	teaspoon salt
2	eggs, beaten	4	cups un-sifted flour

In ¼ cup warm water dissolve package of yeast. Add sugar, eggs and 1 cup warm water. Add oil, salt and flour. Let stand for 8 hours or overnight. Divide in 3 parts; roll out as if you were making pie crust. Cut into 8 sections (like the shape of pie pieces). Roll wide edge into the point, like crescent rolls, and place on greased cookie sheet. Let rise for at least 6 hours. Bake at 375 degrees for 10 to 12 minutes.

Trivia: How did John Berendt find out about the shooting?
(#51)

GRANNY D'S ZUCCHINI BREAD

(From the kitchen of Deb's 97 year young grandmother
Florence Dimick)

2	eggs	1	cup grated zucchini
1	cup sugar	1 ½	cups flour
½	cup oil	½	teaspoon salt
1	teaspoon vanilla	½	teaspoon baking soda
⅛	teaspoon baking powder	1 ½	teaspoons cinnamon
½			cup walnuts

In a mixing bowl beat eggs well; beat in sugar. Stir in oil, zucchini and vanilla, mixing together well. Add dry ingredients and mix thoroughly. Bake at 350 degrees for 1 hour; after removing from oven leave in pan at least 10 minutes before removing. Using 3x5 loaf pans, recipe makes 2 loaves.

One thing I've leaned in growing old
No doubt you've noticed too:
The kids to whom you gave advice
Now give advice to you.

GEORGIA PEANUT BUTTER BISCUITS

(From the Kitchen of Margaret Debolt &
Georgia Peanut Committee)

⅔	cup milk
¼	cup peanut butter
2	cups package biscuit mix
3	slices bacon, cooked and crumbled

Preheat oven to 400 degrees. Place milk and peanut butter in a deep bowl or blender container. Beat at high speed until smooth and well blended. Combine biscuit mix and bacon. Stir lightly. Add milk and peanut butter mixture all at once and stir with fork until dough clings together. Turn out onto a lightly floured board and knead gently a few times. Pat out to about ¾-inch thickness with floured hands. Cut into 2-inch rounds. Bake on a non-greased cookie sheet for 10 to 12 minutes, or until lightly browned.

Peanut Fact: Peanuts were known in South America over two thousand years ago and are believed to be native to Brazil. The ancient pre-Incan tribes buried their dead with peanuts to give them strength on their long voyage through eternity. These tribes also depicted the peanut on their pottery. The Spanish later took peanuts to Europe, and thence they spread to Asia and Africa. Early Virginians fed them to their hogs, producing particularly delicious pork products. Peanuts became an important agricultural crop in the South after The War between the States.

Peanuts are one of the most important cash crops in Georgia. The state leads the nation in the production of peanuts, of which the largest share goes into the production of peanut butter.

EDNA'S COLE SLAW
(From the kitchen of Deb's Great Aunt, Edna
Sioux Falls, South Dakota)

1	medium size cabbage	½	cup vinegar, white
½	cup onion, chopped	1	teaspoon salt
½	cup celery	1	teaspoon celery seed
1 ½	cups sugar	1	teaspoon mustard seed

In a blender *chop-up cabbage. Pour in boiling water, enough to cover cabbage and let stand for 5 minutes. Drain into colander (really drain good); pour into large bowl then mix in remaining ingredients.

Note: Eat as is or cool in refrigerator. Very Good.

* This is an older recipe and Aunt Edna did not own a cuisinart and used her new blender instead.

EDNA'S POTATO SALAD
(Another from the kitchen of Aunt Edna)

6-8   medium potatoes
2   tablespoons Miracle dressing (good)
1   teaspoon mustard
2   tablespoons vinegar
4   heaping teaspoons sugar
1   medium onion, chopped
4-6   boiled eggs

In a large enough bowl to hold ingredients mix all together. Ready to serve or refrigerate.

Trivia: What caused Vera Dutton Strong to make a reservation for Easter Sunday dinner with the Chatham Club? (#54)

DOT'S FRUIT SALAD

3   apples cored, peeled
       and diced
2-3   bananas
1   jar cherries, drained

⅓   cup raisins (optional)
1   cup mini marshmallows
½   cup mayonnaise

       cut in halves

After cutting up fruit into bite-size pieces, place into a bowl mixingaltogether. Mix in remaining ingredients.

Note: When I was growing up, our housekeeper, Dot, would make this salad, but she could never really get the kids to eat it. So instead of the mayonnaise she would substitute Cool whip and that is all it took. When I made this for our children, I would use Cool whip also. This is a great way to get them to eat their fruit and a wonderful after school snack as well.

PAULA'S 5 CUP FRUIT SALAD
(From the kitchen of Paul Kelly Rogers)

1	cup fruit cocktail, drained	1	cup mini marshmallows
1	cup mandarin oranges	1	cup coconut
1	cup Cool Whip or sour cream		

Combine all ingredients in large bowl. Refrigerate. Serve cool.

*Most girls are looking for a man who is
tall, dark and has some.*

GERMAN LUGAR
GERMAN POTATO SALAD
(Even though we are not German, I love this salad)

5	pounds new red potatoes	½	cup water
1	pound bacon		Salt and pepper taste
1½	pounds yellow onion, chopped	2	tablespoons parsley
1½	cups white vinegar		

Peel and dice potatoes; place potatoes in a large pot and add enough water to cover; bring to a boil. While potatoes are boiling, fry bacon until crispy then place onto a paper towel; save drippings. Sauté onions until clear in bacon pan with drippings and bacon remnants. Add vinegar and water and bring to a boil. Drain potatoes and place in a large pan or bowl. Pour drippings with onions over potatoes; add salt, pepper and parsley, mixing altogether well. Serve hot.

Note: If you have any left over the next day, it can be reheated or served cold.

7-UP JELLO SALAD
(From the kitchen of Deborah's late
Aunt Charlotte Dimick, Beaverton, Oregon)

2	3 ounce Jello (lime)	2	cups boiling water
2	3 ounce cream cheese, softened	2	cups cold 7-up

Dissolve Jello in boiling water. Beat in cream cheese, gently add in 7-up; let set. Serve after Jello firms-up.

Trivia: Which Ardsley Park resident experienced a "divine intervention" and what was the life changing message? (#55)

MINERVA'S CHITLINS

Chitlins are an old, old Gullah favorite for a special event or holiday. Chitlins can be purchased from a slaughter house or some Farmers markets. The secret to "chitlins" *is da way you cleans um; verrrry thorough.*

1	gallon "chitlins"		bout a teaspoon salt
3	strips fatback bacon	½	teaspoon peppa
2	small onions, chopped	½	teaspoon minced garlic
1	green bell peppa, chopped	2	cups warm water

Firs thing you do is to clean dem chitlins real good. Fry up dat fatback in a pot, but leave dat grease in dar; when it done turn down da heat and add dem chitlins, onions, bell peppa, salt & peppa and galic. Stir fry ova medium heat for bout 10 minites. Add da warm water and let it just simmer der, stirring casionally fo bout 1 hour.
    I eats um by da bowl full good and hot, yum, yum!

Trivia: What did Minerva ask for at the grave of her deceased common-law husband? (#40)

SAVANNAH OASIS PEPPER STEAK

1	boneless beef steak approximately 1 ½ pounds	4	tablespoons soy sauce
1 ½	ounces oil	1	bay leaf, crushed
1	medium onion, thinly sliced	½	teaspoon basil
2	stocks celery, cut in 2 inch lengths	1	bell pepper, sliced
1 - 1 ½	cups beef bouillon	1	tablespoon cornstarch, mixed with ½ cup water
½	teaspoon Worcestershire sauce		Salt and pepper to taste

Cut steak into ¼ inch thick slices. In a large skillet sauté onion and celery in oil until tender; add meat and brown over high heat. Stir in bouillon, Worcestershire, soy sauce, bay leaf and basil. Reduce heat to low; cover, and simmer until meat is almost tender. Add bell pepper and simmer for 10 to 15 minutes, stirring occasionally. Stir in cornstarch and water; cook until mixture thickens; salt and pepper to taste. Serve with rice, roasted potatoes or potato gratin.

Trivia: What kind of car did Danny Hansford drive? (#42)

HUNTER'S ARMY RANGERS CASSEROLE

*(We salute our brave men and women stationed at
Hunter Army Airfield, Savannah, Georgia)*

1	pound ground round steak	1	cup Vidalia onions, sliced
½	cup green pepper, diced	1	can tomatoes
1	can tomato sauce	½	cup uncooked rice
1	teaspoon chili powder	½	teaspoon hot sauce
	Salt and pepper to taste	½	cup celery, diced

Brown meat; add all other ingredients and bring to a boil. Pour into greased casserole dish. Cover and bake at 350 degrees for about 1 hour or until rice is tender. Add more liquid if necessary.

GRANDMA ALTON'S CHICKEN CASSEROLE

(This is from the kitchen of my sister, Sharon)

1	8 ounce package cornbread stuffing mix (I use Pepperidge Farm)
½	cup melted butter or margarine
2	cups diced cooked chicken
2	cups chicken broth
1	10 ¾ ounce can cream of chicken soup
1	10 ¾ ounce can cream of celery soup

Preheat oven to 350 degrees.
Combine stuffing and butter, mix until blended. Spread some in bottom of lightly greased shallow baking pan. Cover with layer of chicken. Combine broth and soups in sauce pan. Mix well, cook 5 minutes or until heated; spoon mixture evenly over chicken in baking pan. Repeat layers of stuffing and chicken until all are used, ending with stuffing. Bake for 45 minutes or until done.

Note: This is one of my favorite chicken casseroles. It is probably the first dish my sister learned how to fix and fix it well, she does!

CRAB CAKES WITH LEMON DILL SAUCE

(From the kitchen of Martha Giddens Nesbit)

1	tablespoon butter	½	cup bread crumbs
1	green onion, finely chopped	1	egg
2	teaspoons red bell pepper, finely chopped	½	teaspoon minced parsley
1	clove garlic, minced	1	pound white or claw crabmeat, picked through for shells
3	tablespoons heavy cream		
1	tablespoon Dijon mustard		Cayenne pepper, to taste

TOPPING:

½	cup bread crumbs	¼	cup grated Parmesan
2	tablespoons vegetable oil	2	tablespoons butter

Sauté onion, garlic and bell pepper in butter until pepper is limp, about 3 minutes. Add cayenne, cream and mustard. Mix well. Gently fold in crab.

Form into eight patties, about ½-inch thick. Combine bread crumbs and Parmesan cheese; pat topping onto both sides of the patties. Refrigerate until firm, about 2 hours.

Combine the oil and butter in heavy-bottomed or electric skillet. Sauté crab cakes in hot oil/butter mixture for about 3 minutes on each side. Or, place patties cookie sheet, dribble with oil and butter mixture. Bake at 400 degrees for 7 to 10 minutes.

Serve with lemon dill sauce.

LEMON DILL SAUCE

1	cup mayonnaise	1	tablespoon grated lemon peel
¼	cup buttermilk		
2	teaspoons fresh lemon juice	2	tablespoons chopped fresh dill
1	tablespoon minced parsley		
1	small garlic clove, minced		

Combine all ingredients in a bowl and stir well. Refrigerate until chilled; the sauce will thicken as it chills.

SHANE'S DEVILED CRAB

⅓	cup green pepper, diced
½	cup Vidalia onion, diced
¼	cup celery, diced
1	pimento, diced
1	teaspoon salt
½	teaspoon pepper
1	teaspoon seafood seasoning *
1	teaspoon thyme
1	teaspoon Worcestershire sauce
¼	teaspoon Tabasco sauce (or a little more if you like hot)
½	teaspoon dry mustard
¼	cup butter
½	cup flour
2	cups milk
2	pounds crabmeat, picked over well *
	Bread crumbs
	Butter
1	fresh lemon

Melt butter in a saucepan. Add green pepper, onion, celery, pimento, and seasonings and cook over low heat for 10 minutes. Add flour and stir until smooth. Cook another 5 minutes, stirring constantly. Add milk and stir until sauce becomes thick. Stir in crabmeat; spoon in shells or individual ramekins. Sprinkle with bread crumbs and pat with butter. Bake at 400 degrees for about 20 minutes or until a nice golden brown.

Quarter a lemon to squeeze out over crab.

* Old Savannah Seafood seasoning and canned crabmeat may be purchased from "The Book" Gift Shop (912) 233-3867.

Trivia: Who was the founder of Georgia? (#56)

MICHAEL'S LOW COUNTRY BOIL

Seafood, Sullivan style
(From the Boat and to the kitchen of Michael Sullivan)

1	can seafood seasoning*	20	half ears of corn
20-	25 red potatoes	5-6	pounds fresh shrimp
40	2 inch pieces sausage	2-3	Vidalia onions

In a large pot add enough water to cover all ingredients, usually about ⅔ full. Bring to a boil; add seasoning, potatoes and sausage. Reduce heat to medium and cook for about 20 minutes. Add onions and let cook for 10 minutes. Add corn and cook for an additional 10 minutes. Add shrimp, only allowing them to turn nice and pink; do not overcook, 4 to 5 minutes at the most. Remove from stove, drain, through out onto newspaper-covered table and watch everyone go wild! Use Tarter sauce (see recipe) and Cocktail sauce (see recipe). Quarter lemons to squeeze over seafood. Mrs. Wilkes' Hush Puppies (see recipe) are also great to serve with this or try our Gullah 'hush dem puppies' package**. Serves 10.

Note: We like to figure about two potatoes per person, four 2-inch pieces of sausage, two ears of corn and ½-pound of shrimp per person. We use hot, mild or smokey sausage and cut-up to 2-3-inches each. If any leftovers, refrigerate and heat-up the next day.

(If you are coming to Savannah for a convention, party or family reunion and desire a catered Low County affair give contact Shane Sullivan at (912)355-5245 or email us at birdgirl10@prodigy.net)

* Old Savannah seasoning may be purchased from "The Book" Gift Shop.
** Hush dem puppies mix can be purchased from "The Book" Gift Shop. Very easy to use, just add water.

Trivia: Who crashed the Black Debutante ball? (#24)

CAROLYN'S SHRIMP DIP

(From the kitchen of my sister-in-law Carolyn Sullivan Savannah, Georgia)

1	pound fresh shrimp Salt to taste
1	8 ounce package cream cheese
	Squirt of mustard (optional)
1	(not quite) cup mayonnaise
	Dash of parsley
1	medium onion, finely chopped

Fill a medium pot halfway with water, bring to a boil; add shrimp and boil until they turn a nice pink, usually 2 to 3 minutes. Drain and set aside. In a bowl combine ingredients and mix until smooth. Once shrimp have cooled peel and devein. Cut into either halves or if larger shrimp, cut into thirds; add to mixture, combine well. Chill and serve with crackers or spread onto bread and serve as sandwiches.

CAROLYN'S COCKTAIL SAUCE

2	cups ketchup		Juice of 1 lemon
2	tablespoons horseradish	½	teaspoon Tabasco or
2	tablespoons Worcestershire sauce		hot sauce

Blend together all ingredients. Add more of any to your taste. Serve right away or refrigerate for later use.

Note: We brown-up our sauce with more Worcestershire, but you may like it a little spicier; add horseradish and/or Tabasco sauce.

Trivia: What magazine featured six full pages of the Mercer House? (#59)

CAROLYN'S TARTER SAUCE

(From the kitchen of Carolyn Sullivan
Savannah, Georgia)

1	jar Hellmann's mayonnaise
	Juice of whole lemon
1	medium-large onion, finely chopped
	Squirt of yellow mustard (for taste & coloring)
1	12 ounce jar sweet pickle relish
	Pepper to taste
	Sprinkle of garlic powder

In a large bowl combine all ingredients and mix together thoroughly. Since this makes a good bit of tarter sauce, put some up in several jars or be a good neighbor and give some away.

Note: We use this with just about all our seafood and after tasting it I'm convinced that you will too.

Trivia: What on Victory Drive serves as a memorial to soldiers from Georgia who died during World War I? (#68)

SOUTHERN SEAFOOD GUMBO

(From the kitchen of Louise Streed)

4	tablespoons vegetable oil
4	tablespoons all-purpose flour
3	tablespoons butter
1	large onion, medium chopped
3	large cloves garlic, minced
1	quart water, plus 2 cups
4-5	dashes Tabasco hot sauce
3	tablespoons Worcestershire sauce
3-4	bay leaves
1½	teaspoons salt
½	teaspoon black pepper
¾	pounds fresh or frozen cut okra
½	pound fresh or frozen crabmeat (preferably back fin)
¾	pounds fresh or thawed frozen shrimp
1	pint fresh oysters, drained
	Filé powder, optional

Over medium heat, combine flour and vegetable oil to make roux. Roux is important; stir constantly until color becomes the color of a penny, do not heat too high or roux will be bitter. Melt butter in a skillet, add onion, (you may want to add some chopped green peppers and/or chopped celery); cook until tender. Stir in roux and gradually add water and garlic, Worcestershire sauce, hot sauce, bay leaves, salt to taste and add pepper. After all water has been added, put in okra, add crabmeat and simmer 30 minutes. Stir in shrimp and oysters; cook 10 minutes more.

Serve in bowls with ½ teaspoon filé powder in bottom of bowl, add cooked rice and pour Gumbo over rice and enjoy.

Trivia: John Berendt divided his time in Savannah with what other location? (#38)

Hamilton-Turner House
Savannah, Georgia

Pamela Lee © 2000

SHANE'S BRUNSWICK STEW

1	1 -1 ½ pounds cooked pork	1	Vidalia onion, chopped
1	28 ounce can crushed tomatoes, sweetened with ½ cup sugar	1	tablespoon vinegar Salt & pepper to taste Celery salt to taste
1	16 ounce can creamed corn		
1	cup ketchup		
1	tablespoon liquid smoke		
½	cup (your favorite) barbeque sauce		

I usually get an extra 1 or 2 pounds of meat when I go out (I like my stew a little meatier), and one of my favorite places in Savannah is Johnny Harris Restaurant. Chop up meat; in a stock pot, mix meat and all other ingredients. Simmer slowly for about 30 minutes, stirring often to prevent sticking. If stew gets too thick add a little chicken stock. This is great by itself or served over rice. Any left over meat is great as a sandwich.

You can buy flattery but envy must be earned

SHANIE'S PIGSKIN FILETS

(Hot off the grill from our son, Shane, Jr.
Sugar Hill, Georgia)

4	Choice Cut USDA grain-fed Filet Steak
½	cup Jack Daniels Bourbon Whiskey
¼	cup Lea & Perrin's Worcestershire sauce
	Garlic salt to taste
	Fresh crushed black pepper
4	slices hickory-flavored bacon, cut in halves

MARINATE:

Make a marinating liquid by combining ½ cup Jack Daniels and ¼ cup Worcestershire sauce.

Place bacon strips on bottom of a sealable container. Place filets on top of bacon strips. Using a fork, tenderize steak by poking plenty of holes in each of the filets. Slowly pour marinate over filets allowing it to pool on top of steaks. Sprinkle with garlic and fresh pepper. Refrigerate overnight turning filets over once (don't forget to sprinkle garlic salt and pepper on the flip side); then re-cover.

Warm the grill and grab the filets. Place bacon directly on grill and cook filets on top of the bacon. Cook to your liking.

Note: Perfect for tailgating on one of the "High Holidays," the annual Georgia-Florida Football Game. Joe would be proud of this recipe, but he would probably add a little more 'JD' but would think it sacrilege to pull against the dawgs.

Serves 4.

DON'T FORGET TO PULL FOR THE GATORS!!!

Trivia: Who tangoed to police headquarters? (#13)

LISA'S CHEESY TATERS

(From the kitchen of Lisa Sullivan
Sugar Hill, Georgia)

8-10   new potatoes, quartered (peeled if you like)
1   block of Pepper Jack cheese, grated
4   slices hickory bacon

Boil potatoes until soft; place in a casserole dish. Spread grated cheese over potatoes and place in a preheated 300 degree oven until cheese melts. Fry up bacon until crisp. When potatoes are done, remove from oven and sprinkle bacon over top. Salt and pepper to taste and serve hot. **Note:** Great with steaks.

Serves 4.

BAKED GARLIC CHEESE GRITS

1	cup regular grits, uncooked	4	cups water
2	teaspoons salt	½	cup butter or margarine
1	garlic clove, minced		Dash of hot sauce
8	ounces grated sharp		(optional)
	Cheddar cheese	2	eggs, lightly beaten
1	tablespoon Worcestershire sauce		

Cook grits in salted water. Add butter, garlic, Worcestershire sauce, hot sauce (if using) and Cheddar cheese. Add a small amount of hot grits to eggs to temper them; add eggs to rest of grits. Stir well.

Pour into buttered casserole dish and bake at 350 degrees for 45 to 50 minutes, until set. If desired, top casserole with thin cheese slices in pattern, which will melt in the last few minutes if cooking.

Serves 8 to 10 as side dish.

POTATOES AU GRATIN

1	cup milk	Dash nutmeg, freshly grated
1	cup heavy cream	Salt and pepper to taste
1	garlic clove, minced	
2	tablespoons butter	
4	russet potatoes (approximately 2 pounds) scrubbed and dried	

Preheat oven to 375 degrees. In a medium saucepan combine milk, cream, garlic, butter, nutmeg, salt and pepper. Peel and thinly slice potatoes. Add potatoes to milk mixture and simmer over medium heat, stirring occasionally. Cover and cook for about 3 minutes. With a slotted spoon, place potatoes into a casserole dish, arranging in overlapping layers. Pour mixture over potatoes, cover, and bake for 30 minutes. Uncover dish and bake until potatoes are tender, and the top is brown and crusty, about 20 minutes more; liquid should be thick and bubbling.

Remove from oven and let stand for about 10 minutes before serving.

Trivia: Where did the last trial take place? (#43)

OKRA AND TOMATOES

4 slices hickory-smoked bacon
1 pound fresh okra, ends trimmed and sliced
  Salt and cayenne pepper
½ cup chicken broth
1 large onion, chopped
5 ripe tomatoes, peeled and chopped (or 1 large can whole peeled tomatoes, chopped with juice)

Sauté bacon until crisp; remove bacon from skillet and crumble. Add onion to bacon grease and cook until soft, about 3 minutes. Add okra and sauté for a minute in bacon fat. Add tomatoes and seasonings. Reduce heat. Simmer until okra is tender, about 20 minutes. Add chicken broth if mixture becomes too thick. Add crumbled bacon immediately before serving.

Serves 6 to 8 as part of a large meal.

BETH'S MUSHROOM SAUCE
(From the kitchen of Beth Sullivan, my sister-in-law Crystal River, Florida)

6 tablespoons margarine only (not butter)
1 large can Green Giant sliced or button mushrooms
4 tablespoons Worcestershire sauce (I use Lea & Perrins)

Mclt margarine in a skillet. Add Worcestershire sauce. Before you are ready to serve add mushrooms; simmer over low heat for 4-5 minutes. Serve as a side or on top of steaks.

Note: This is a delicious sauce to serve over your favorite steak.

Fun Fact: John Berendt wrote for the Esquire magazine and served as editor for New York magazine.

DEB'S SWEET POTATO SOUFFLÉ

(From the kitchen of Deborah Sullivan)

3	cups sweet potatoes	½	teaspoon salt
1	cup sugar	2	eggs
¼	cup flour	1	teaspoon vanilla butter-nut flavoring
¼	cup fresh orange juice		
⅓	cup milk	¼	cup butter

In a large bowl mash potatoes; mix in all other ingredients, blending together thoroughly. Pour into a casserole dish and add topping (see below).

TOPPING:

1	cup brown sugar
⅓	cup all-purpose flour
⅓	cup butter
1	cup pecans, chopped

Mix sugar and butter together; add flour and pecans. Spread over top of potato mixture and bake at 350 degrees for 40 to 45 minutes.

Note: You may substitute marshmallows for brown sugar. When soufflé is just about finished cooking, place marshmallows on top and cook until they brown.

Trivia: For what family was the Bird Girl sculpted in the 1930s? (#80)

DEB'S SWEET BAKED BEAN CASSEROLE

1	Vidalia onion, sliced *	½	bell pepper
2	cups ground beef	2	1 pound cans Bush
1	tablespoon mustard		brown sugar baked
3	tablespoons brown sugar		beans
1	teaspoon salt	1	tablespoon cherry juice
2	tablespoons Vidalia Onion BBQ sauce **		

Preheat oven to 400 degrees. In a skillet sauté onions and bell pepper until tender; place in a 2 quart casserole dish. Brown hamburger meat; drain, mix into casserole dish with onions and bell pepper. Mix in remaining ingredients and blend well. Bake covered for 30-35 minutes; uncover and bake an additional 5 minutes.

Note: Deb will sometimes add ¼ cup of ground chuck. I will add cut-up steak from dinner the night before if we have any leftover.

* We use Vidalia onions, but you can use your grocery store's brand.
** Vidalia Onion BBQ sauce may be purchased from "The Book" Gift Shop or you may use your favorite brand sauce.

Trivia: What was built in Bonaventure Cemetery in honor of William Gaston, who was one of Savannah's best nineteenth century hosts? (#78)

MS. EMMA'S CROCK OF BEANS
(From the kitchen of Emma Kelly)

1 ½	pounds ground beef	1	64 ounce can pork and
1	cup chopped onions		beans
2	teaspoons vinegar	⅓	cup brown sugar
	Kraft hickory barbeque sauce		

Brown meat and onions; drain. Combine meat and onions with other ingredients in crock pot. Add barbeque sauce to taste.
Cook on high for 2 hours or low for 4 hours.

FLORENCE SCALLOPED CORN

(From the kitchen of Florence Dimick)

2	cans creamed corn	1 ¼	cup cracker crumbs
2	cans whole corn	1	small onion, minced
1	can evaporated milk	1	egg, beaten
2	tablespoons butter, melted		

In a large enough bowl mix all ingredients together and pour into a buttered pan. Bake at 350 degrees for about 30 minutes or maybe a little longer.

Trivia: What song would Emma play to signal Joe Odom to take over at the piano? Hint: It's also a chapter title in "The Book." (#81)

FORSYTH PARK PICNIC COOKIES

2 ½	cups oatmeal	½	teaspoon salt
2	sticks butter	1	teaspoon baking powder
1	cup sugar	1	teaspoon baking soda
1	cup brown sugar	12	ounces chocolate chips
2	eggs	4	ounces Hershey bar, grated
1	teaspoon vanilla		
2	cups flour	1 ½	cups chopped nuts

In a blender pour oatmeal and mix into a fine powder. Cream together butter and both sugars; add eggs and vanilla. Mix together with flour, oatmeal, salt, baking powder, and baking soda. Add chips, candy bar and nuts. Roll into a ball and place onto a cookie sheet, about 2-inches apart. Bake at 375 degrees for about 6 minutes.

Makes about 60 cookies.

YANKEE LACE OATMEAL COOKIES
(From the oven of Diane Phillips, Atlanta, Georgia)

2	cups quick cooked oatmeal	5	tablespoons flour
2	cups sugar	½	pound melted butter
1	teaspoon salt	2	eggs, well beaten
½	teaspoon baking powder	4	teaspoons vanilla

Mix dry ingredients, pour melted butter over mix; add eggs and vanilla. Stir well until blended. Let stand 20 minutes until thickened. Cover baking trays with foil. Place ½ teaspoon of batter at least 2 inches apart on foil. Bake at 300 degrees for 8 to 10 minutes. Leave on foil until cool; then peel off.

Approximately 4 dozen cookies.

GRANDMA'S OATMEAL CINNAMON COOKIES OR DROPS
(A favorite recipe from the kitchen of Florence Dimick)
Thanks Grandma. We love and miss you

1	cup (2 sticks) butter	2	teaspoons cinnamon
2	cups sugar	1 ½	teaspoons baking soda
2	eggs	2	cups oatmeal
1	tablespoon molasses	1	cup nuts (walnuts, pecans etc, chopped)
2	teaspoons vanilla		
2	cups flour	½	cup chocolate chips

In a mixing bowl, cream butter and sugar together; add eggs, molasses and vanilla. Set aside. In another bowl combine flour, cinnamon and baking soda; gradually add to cream mixture. Stir in oatmeal, nuts and chocolate chips until consistent. Drop by teaspoon onto non-greased cookie sheet, baking at 350 degrees for about 10 to 12 minutes.

7-LAYER COOKIES

(From the kitchen of Sharon Stewart,
Beaufort, South Carolina)

1   block of butter, melted
1   cup graham crackers, crumbled
1   6 ounce package of chocolate chips
1   6 ounce package of butterscotch chips
1   cup coconut
1   cup crushed pecans
1   can sweetened condensed milk

Pour butter into bottom of brownie pan. Layer all ingredients, do not mix, starting with crackers, then chips, and coconut. Once through layering, pour condensed milk over carefully and evenly; add pecans. Bake at 325 to 350 degrees for 25 to 30 minutes. Cool before cutting.

Note: Warning! These are not for the dieter, but they are soooo gooood.

The trouble with the younger generation is that
it hasn't read the minutes of the last meeting.

Trivia: What could happen only on the ride to Tybee Island but not on the ride from Tybee Island? (#25)

PEARL'S SUGAR COOKIES

*(From the kitchen of Grandma Dimick's good friend
Pearl Nelson, Beaverton, Oregon)*

3	cups flour	1	teaspoon baking soda
1	cup sugar	½	teaspoon salt
1	teaspoon cream of tartar	2	eggs, beaten
1 ¼	cups shortening	3	tablespoons milk
		1	teaspoon vanilla

Mix flour, sugar, tartar, shortening, and baking soda together as if making a pie crust. Add eggs, milk and vanilla; mixing together thoroughly. Roll into balls, spread-out with bottom of glass. Place onto baking sheet, sprinkle with a little sugar and bake at 350 degrees for 10 minutes.

GINGER COOKIES

*(From the kitchen of Grandma Westaby,
Deborah's Great Grandmother)*

1	cup white sugar	1	teaspoon salt
1	cup brown sugar	½	teaspoon cloves
1	cup shortening	1	teaspoon ginger
1	cup molasses	2	teaspoons cinnamon
1	egg	5	cups flour
1	teaspoon baking soda	½	cup hot water

ICING

1	cup sugar	1	egg white
¼	cup water	½	tablespoon vanilla

Put sugar, water and unbeaten egg white in pan and cook over boiling water. Beat with beater until frosting is proper to spread; add vanilla

Trivia: What Statesboro, Georgia native and Savannah favorite was generally allowed to do eighty or ninety on Georgia Highways? (#69)

GRANDMA ROVOLIS' KOULORAKIA
(Greek Cookies)

½	pound butter
4	eggs
2	pounds (or 8 cups) flour, sifted
1	pound (or 2 ¼ cups) sugar
1 ½	teaspoons baking soda
1 ½	teaspoons baking powder
¾	cup milk
¼	teaspoon nutmeg
1	teaspoon cinnamon
⅛	teaspoon lemon
2	teaspoons vanilla sesame seeds

Beat butter slightly; add sugar and mix until creamy, add eggs one at a time. In another bowl combine sifted flour, baking soda and baking powder together; then mix slowly with butter and sugar mixture, add milk and spices. Mixture will become a dough. Take out a small amount; roll out into about a 5 to 6-inch long, ½-inch thick pencil-like tube on lightly floured wax paper, then twist. Brush on a light amount of egg wash and sprinkle with sesame seeds. Set out on baking sheet, place in preheated oven at 350 degrees for about 20 minutes or lightly brown. Great warm with cold glass of milk or cool, dunked in coffee.

Makes about 7 dozen.

CHOCOLATE MINT BALLS

1 ½   cups sugar
¾   cup margarine
1   5 ounce can evaporated milk
2   packages Andes mints
1   7 ounce jar marshmallows
1   teaspoon vanilla
22   ounces white baking chocolate
½   cup semisweet chocolate chips

Combine sugar, margarine, and milk; bring to a boil on medium heat until candy thermometer reads 236 degrees. Remove from heat, stir in Andes mints, marshmallow cream, and vanilla. Spread mixture into pan and refrigerate for 1 hour. Cut into small squares and roll into balls; freeze for just a couple of minutes on wax paper.

Melt white chocolate and chocolate chips; dip balls into chocolate mixture or if you would like to decorate, save some of the white chocolate and drizzle over balls.

Trivia: What was the name of the newly elected District Attorney? (#85)

Fun Fact: Spencer Lawton is still the District Attorney at the 1st printing of this cookbook.

PEANUT BUTTER POPCORN
(From the kitchen of Deb's late aunt
Charlotte Dimick, Beaverton, Oregon)

½   cup popped corn

COATING MIXTURE:

¼   pound butter, melted   20   marshmallows
¾   cup brown sugar   ¼   cup peanut butter (you
                                        may want to add a little
                                        more)

In a saucepan, melt butter; add sugar, marshmallows and peanut butter, mixing thoroughly. Pour over popcorn.

Note: Great to make ahead and snack on while traveling; one of Shane's favorites.

Trivia: What part of Jim Williams's apparel seemed odd in Mercer House according to John Berendt? (#67)

EMMA'S SWEET POTATO BALLS
(From the kitchen of the late Emma Kelly)

2   cups mashed sweet potatoes   12   large marshmallows
¾   cup finely crushed   ½   cup brown sugar, packed
     corn flakes   2   tablespoons milk
¼   cup oleo or butter

Mold a spoonful of potatoes around each marshmallow; then roll in cornflakes. Place balls in a shallow 1 ½ quart baking dish. In a saucepan bring to a boil sugar, milk and oleo. Pour over balls and bake uncovered for 15 minutes at 350 degrees.

PECAN TASSIES

(From the kitchen of Martha Giddens Nesbit)

PASTRY:

3 ounces softened cream cheese

1 cup all-purpose flour

½ cup softened butter

¼ teaspoon salt

FILLING:

1 egg, beaten

2 tablespoons softened butter

1 teaspoon vanilla

¾ cup brown sugar

¼ teaspoon salt

1 cup finely chopped pecans

Mix pastry ingredients until blended. Chill. Form pastry into 2 balls; press with hands into bottom and up sides of non-greased miniature muffin tins.

For filling, beat together all ingredients except pecans.

Sprinkle a few nuts in the bottom of each pastry shell. Pour filling over nuts, filling each tin ¾ full.

Bake at 350 degrees for 20 to 25 minutes; or until filling is set.

Cool slightly; remove from muffin tins by running knife around edges. Cool on wire racks. Store in tightly covered container.

Makes 24. Can be frozen.

Trivia: What did Luther Drigger's breakfast always consist of? (#72)

Pamela Lee

GEORGIA PECAN CLUSTERS
(From the kitchen of Martha Giddens Nesbit)

1	egg white, beaten stiffly	1	cup dark or light brown sugar
2	cups pecans, coarsely chopped or broken into large pieces		

Preheat oven to 450 degrees. Beat egg white until stiff. Add brown sugar and beat for 30 seconds, until blended. Mix in nuts with spoon, saving 2 to 3 tablespoons to add at end when batter is low on nuts. Drop by teaspoonfuls on greased cookie sheets at least 1 inch apart.

Turn off oven and place pans in oven. Let stand at least 1 hour before opening oven. Let cool and crisp on rack. Store in air-tight container. Makes 18 to 24.

Trivia: What medical condition did Jim Williams suffer from? (#62)

MRS. SULLIVAN'S BENNE WAFERS

1	pound light brown sugar
2	eggs
1	teaspoon baking powder
2	teaspoons vanilla
3	sticks butter
2	cups all-purpose flour
¼	teaspoon salt
1 ½	cups toasted sesame seeds

To toast sesame seeds: Place seeds in single layer on cookie sheet. Place in 350 degree oven for about 5 minutes, watching carefully. They should just begin to lightly brown. Or, purchase already toasted seeds.

Cream the first three ingredients. Sift flour, baking powder and salt. Add to butter mixture. Stir until combined. Add vanilla. Stir in sesame seeds. Drop by ½ teaspoon on wax paper on cookie sheet. Cook at 300 degrees until brown, about 14 minutes. Cookies must be very brown, but not burned on the edges.

Important: let cool completely on wax paper, then peel away from paper. Store in airtight container.

Makes about 12 dozen. Wafers freeze well.

Fun Fact: The Mercer House was used in the filming of *Midnight in the Garden of Good and Evil*. This included the Christmas party scene and a number of shots with Jim Williams, played by Kevin Spacey, and John Kelso, played by John Cusack.

PINEAPPLE BAKE

(From the kitchen of our good friends Ron & Kay Walker)

4	slices white bread, remove crust
3	eggs, beaten
½	cup sugar
2	teaspoons flour
	Pinch of salt
1	14 ounce can crushed pineapple (do not drain)
1	stick butter or margarine

Tear bread into pieces. Mix bread, eggs, sugar, flour, salt and pineapple. Pour into a greased 1 ½ quart casserole dish. Slice butter into pieces and evenly drop on top of mixture. Bake for 45 minutes in a 350 degree oven.

Trivia: What item did Minerva instruct Jim Williams to bring with him for their visit to the graveyard in Beaufort? (#39)

"THE BOOK" CALHOUN SQUARES

(This is from Deborah's brother, Donnie Dimick, who now owns "The Cake Corner" in Pooler, Georgia)

1	stick butter	1	egg
1	box Duncan Hines butter	1	teaspoon vanilla butter-nut recipe cake mix flavoring
½	cup pecans, finely chopped		

Preheat oven to 350 degrees. Mix butter, egg, cake mix, vanilla and pecans together well: press into a greased 9x13x2-inch pan (mixture should be stiff). Before placing into oven add topping (see below).

TOPPING:

1	box powered sugar	1	8 ounce cream cheese
3	medium eggs	1	teaspoon vanilla butter-nut flavoring
½	cup butter		

Mix all ingredients together, pour into pan over top of cake mixture (see above) and bake at 350 degrees for 40-45 minutes or until golden brown. Do not overcook; you want center to be a little gooey.

The family loves these squares. Deborah keeps them in the refrigerator for us; they are delicious cold. Sprinkle them with a little powdered sugar for a nice presentation.

Note: Deborah uses vanilla butter-nut flavoring quite often. You can find it in some grocery stores, but the best flavorings are found in bakeries or upscale kitchen stores. She purchases hers from "The Cake Corner" in Pooler, Georgia – (912) 748-5952.

Trivia: How many squares originally dotted the streets of Savannah? How many are left now? (#53)

WALNUT SQUARES
(From the kitchen of Ron & Kay Walker, Pooler, Georgia)

1	egg, unbeaten
1	cup brown sugar, packed
1	teaspoon vanilla
½	cup sifted all-purpose flour
¼	teaspoon baking soda
¼	teaspoon salt
1	cup coarsely chopped walnuts

Grease an 8-inch square pan. Stir together egg, brown sugar, and vanilla. Quickly stir in flour, baking soda, and salt. Add walnuts. Spread in pan. Bake in preheated 350 degree oven for 18 to 20 minutes. Cut into 2 inch squares.

Yields 16 Walnut Squares.

Trivia: What method did Jim Williams devise when it came time to make out his Christmas part list? (#47)

EMMA'S CHOCOLATE PIANO BARS

1	18-21 ounce brownie mix
1	8 ounce cream cheese, softened

Prepare brownie mix according to instructions on package. Pour into pan; swirl cream cheese into batter before baking. Bake per instructions.

Note: For an unusual treat use a fruit flavored cream cheese; orange or strawberry.

Fun Fact: Emma Kelly had a cameo role playing herself in "The Movie" during the Christmas party scene inside of Mercer House.

EMMA'S CHOCOLATE PIANO BAR COOKIES

1   18-21 ounce brownie mix
1   cup chopped macadamia nuts
²/₃   cup white chocolate chips

Prepare brownie mix according to instructions on package. Add chopped nuts and chips to the batter and drop spoonfuls onto a lightly greased cookie sheet. Bake until crisp at the edges, but soft in the middle; 8 to 10 minutes.

FRUIT PIZZA
(From the kitchen of Kay Walker, Pooler, Georgia)

1   package sugar cookie dough
1   8 ounce package cream cheese, softened
½   cup orange marmalade
2   tablespoons water
½   teaspoon vanilla
⅓   cup sugar
1   large can crushed pineapple, drained
1   banana, sliced
2   packages frozen strawberries, drained
     (any canned, frozen or fresh fruit may be added.
     To make it colorful use blueberries, kiwi,
     cherries, or raspberries)

Mash cookie dough in large pizza pan or jelly roll pan. Bake 12 minutes in a preheated 350 degree oven. Mix cream cheese, sugar, and vanilla and spread on cooled cookie. Top with fruits. Mix water and marmalade and drizzle over fruit. Refrigerate.

Note: Deborah made this for me with blueberries and raspberries and I think I just about ate the whole thing that same day. Delicious!

Trivia: Sonny Seiler and his family are responsible for what famous dogs? (16)

SEVEN MINUTE ICING

2	unbeaten egg whites	1 ½	teaspoons light corn
1 ½	cups sugar		syrup
5	tablespoons cold water	1	teaspoon vanilla extract
¼	teaspoon cream of tartar		

Place egg whites, sugar, water, cream of tartar and corn syrup in top of a double boiler. Beat until thoroughly blended. Place over rapidly boiling water. Beat with electric mixer or rotary beater for 7 minutes. Remove icing from heat and beat in vanilla extract (if icing thickens too quickly while cooking, add a small amount of boiling water.) Continue beating until icing is the proper consistency for spreading.

COKE CHOCOLATE CAKE

4	cups plain flour	4	cups sugar
2	sticks butter or margarine	8	tablespoons cocoa
2	cups coke	1	cup buttermilk
4	eggs, beaten	2	teaspoons baking soda
4	teaspoons vanilla	3	tablespoons cinnamon
1	teaspoon salt	1	pound butter

ICING:

½	cup butter	½	cup coke
6	tablespoons cocoa	1	cup chopped pecans
2	teaspoons vanilla	2	boxes powdered sugar

Grease and flour an 11x17 inch pan. Sift together the dry ingredients and set aside. In a saucepan, heat the butter and coke until the butter melts. Add the eggs, vanilla and buttermilk and mix well. Add the liquid to the dry ingredients and beat until smooth. The batter will be very thin. Pour into the prepared pan and bake at 350 degrees for 30 minutes. This should fill 2 tube pans or 2 paper-lined cupcake tins. Bake tube cakes for 60 minutes; cupcakes for 15 minutes. This cake must be iced while warm.

Icing: In a saucepan, heat the butter and coke. **Do not boil**. Add the remaining ingredients and mix well. Pour over cake.

BANANA SPLIT CAKE
(From the kitchen of Kay Walker, Pooler, Georgia)

2	cups graham cracker crumbs
2	sticks of butter or margarine
5	bananas
2	cups powdered sugar
2	eggs
1	large container Cool Whip
8	chopped maraschino cherries
¼-½	cup chopped nuts
1	large can crushed pineapple, drained

Mix graham cracker crumbs with 1 stick of butter. Cover the bottom of a 9x13x2 inch pan with mixture. Combine sugar, eggs, and 1 stick butter in a large bowl. Beat on high speed for 15 minutes or until creamy. Pour over cracker mixture. Slice and layer bananas over mixture. Cover bananas with pineapple; cover pineapple with Cool Whip.

Top with cherries and nuts. Chill for 24 hours for best results.

Tip: If possible, chill graham cracker mixture for 2-3 hours before adding cake filling.

*Optimism: A cheerful frame of mind that
enables a tea kettle to sing even though
it's in hot water up to its nose*

CHOCOLATE-SINFULLY EVIL-CHOCOLATE-CHOCOLATE CAKE

4	ounces unsweetened baking chocolate, melted	2 ½	cups sifted all-purpose White Lily or cake flour
¾	cup butter	1	teaspoon baking soda
2 ½	cups sugar	1	cup buttermilk
5	eggs, separated	1	teaspoon vanilla extract

Have butter and eggs at room temperature. Grease, line bottom with wax paper, grease paper and flour three 8-inch round cake pans. Preheat oven to 350 degrees. Cream butter and sugar until light and fluffy; beat in egg yolks 1 at a time; beat in melted chocolate. Sift flour and baking soda together. Beat in alternately with buttermilk, starting and ending with flour. Beat in vanilla. Beat egg whites until stiff but not dry. Beat ¼ of the egg whites into chocolate mixture to lighten it, and then fold chocolate mixture into egg whites gently but thoroughly. Chocolate batter is very heavy and doesn't want to cooperate, but be firm. Divide batter among pans, smooth tops and bake for 30 to 35 minutes, until tops spring back when lightly touched and cake shrinks from sides of pan. Cool on wire racks and turn out. You may have to slip finger under the wax paper to get it started. Fill and ice.

FILLING

½	cup sugar	1	cup milk
2	tablespoons flour	1	egg
	Pinch salt	1	tablespoon butter
2	ounces unsweetened baking chocolate	½	teaspoon vanilla extract

Mix dry ingredients. Whisk in egg until smooth. Melt chocolate in milk in a heavy saucepan, stirring constantly. Gradually pour milk into egg mixture, whisking rapidly and constantly. Return mixture to saucepan and cook, stirring constantly with a wooden spoon, until mixture thickens and comes to a boil. Remove from heat; beat in butter and vanilla. Pour into a bowl, place a piece of plastic wrap directly on the surface of the filling and refrigerate until cool. Use between layers of cake.

(See icing mixture recipe, below).

ICING

2	ounces unsweetened baking chocolate	1	cup milk
⅓	cup butter	2	cups sugar
1	teaspoon flour	1	teaspoon vanilla extract

Melt chocolate and butter in a large, heavy saucepan over low heat, stirring constantly. Dissolve flour in part of the milk; add milk, flour and sugar to chocolate. Bring to a boil, stirring frequently, and boil until mixture reaches soft ball stage on a candy thermometer (234 degrees). Remove from heat, stir in vanilla, and beat with an electric mixer until icing becomes just thick enough to spread. Do not let it harden too much. If icing does become too hard, beat in a little milk; ice entire outside of the cake. Dip spatula or knife in hot water to smooth icing.

Note: Do not let the length of this recipe intimidate you. For true chocolate lovers, it is well worth the effort.

When adding flour and liquid to cake batter, add flour in 4 batches and liquid in 3, starting and ending with flour.

Trivia: What house was featured in "A Fields Guide to American Houses? (#66)

COCONUT CRÈME CAKE
(Savannah Style)

1	cup margarine
2	cups sugar
5	eggs, separated
1	teaspoon baking soda
1	cup buttermilk
1	teaspoon vanilla
½	teaspoon salt
1 ½	cups coconut

FROSTING:

1	stick margarine
8	ounce cream cheese, softened
1	16 ounce box powdered sugar
1	teaspoon vanilla
1	cup coconut

Blend margarine and sugar until creamy. Add in egg yolks. Add baking soda and buttermilk. Stir in flour and milk, alternating between each; beginning and ending with flour. Beat egg whites until stiff; add vanilla and salt. Fold whites into batter, then coconut. Pour into three greased and slightly floured 8 or 9-inch pans. Bake at 350 degrees for 30 minutes.

Frosting: Cream margarine and cream cheese. Beat in powdered sugar, add vanilla. Spread frosting over cake and sprinkle coconut on top and sides.

DEB'S LEMON LUSH
(From the kitchen of Deborah Sullivan)

1	stick butter or margarine
1	cup flour
½	cup chopped pecans
1	cup powdered sugar
1	8 ounce package cream cheese, (⅓ less fat)
1	small tub light Cool Whip
23.4	ounce packages instant lemon pudding
3	cups milk

Mix together melted butter, flour, and nuts. Press into bottom of 8-x-12-inch non-greased pan and bake at 350 degrees for 15 to 20 minutes. When dough cools, brush with a little Savannah almond mix*. Combine sugar, cream cheese and 1 cup of Cool Whip and spread over top of crust. Mix pudding with milk until thick; let set, and then spread over cheese layer. Spread on remaining topping, sprinkle with pecans and refrigerate.

Note: This is such a great dessert during the holidays or any special occasion. My brother, Richard, and brother-in-law, Dick, are always fighting for the last bite (Richard has been known to hide a bowl full from everyone else).

* Savannah Almond mix as well as other Savannah mixes may be purchased from "The Book" Gift Shop at (912) 233-3867.

Trivia: What did Jim Williams smoke? (#41)

DIRTY DIRT BY DEB
(Another favorite from the kitchen of Deborah Sullivan)

1   **large bag Oreo cookies, crumbled fine**
1   **large container light Cool Whip**
1   **cup confectioners' sugar**
1   **8 ounce package (⅓ less fat) cream cheese, softened**
2   **cups milk**
2   **small boxes instant vanilla pudding (instant sugar-free will work)**

Put ½ of the crumbled cookies on the bottom of a 9-x-13-inch baking dish or pan. Mix Cool Whip, cream cheese, pudding, and milk; pour over cookie layer. Pour remaining crumbled cookie crumbs on top. Chill for 1 ½ to 2 hours.

Note: While Lemon Lush is a favorite with the older adults, Dirty Dirt is a favorite with our kids, nieces and nephews. Deborah has been creative with this dish from time to time. One year she purchased some small flower pots from a local craft store, cleaned them thoroughly (I guess) and spooned the *dirt* into these pots for individual servings. When the kids were younger, she would hide gummy worms in the pots, as well.

As I said earlier, 'making memories' is what the holiday season or special gatherings with family, is all about for me.

COBBLESTONE PIE

(From the kitchen of Helen Sullivan
Mema's Chocolate Chip Pie)

¾	cup sugar
½	cup all-purpose flour
½	cup melted butter or margarine, cooled
1	egg, beaten slightly
1	teaspoon vanilla extract
1	6 ounce package semisweet chocolate morsels
1	cup pecans, chopped
1	9-inch pastry shell unbaked
	Ice cream or whipped topping (optional)

Combine sugar, flour, butter or margarine, eggs, vanilla, chocolate morsels, and pecans; mixing thoroughly. Pour into unbaked pastry shell; bake at 350 degrees for 35 minutes. Serve warm with ice cream or whipped cream, if desired.

Note: During the Christmas holidays, mom makes up about 10 of these pies; one for each of the families and several extras in case unexpected company drops by. And there is always a troublemaker in each family. My niece, Leigh, insist on having her own pie, without nuts, but mema always obliges since she is the oldest (spoiled) granddaughter.

Fun Fact: The Lady Chablis played herself in "The Movie" *Midnight in the Garden of Good and Evil.*

PEACHY PEACH COBBLER
(From the kitchen of Deborah Sullivan)

4	cups thinly sliced fresh peaches	1	cup butter
1 ½	cups sugar	1	cup self-rising flour
		1	cup milk
			Pinch of salt

Prepare apples or peaches and mix with ½ cup sugar. Melt butter in 2 quart baking dish or 8 ramekins. Mix flour, remaining sugar, and salt. Add milk and mix well. Pour over melted butter. Add fruit on top of this mixture (do not stir) and bake at 350 degrees for about 1 hour or until crust has risen to top and browned. Serve hot with ice cream.

Note: Recipe can also be made with apples instead of peaches; for an apple cobbler.

BANANA PUDDING
(From the kitchen of the late Emma Kelly)

1	box instant vanilla pudding	**MERINGUE**	
1	7 ¼ ounce box Vanilla Wafers	2	egg whites
4	bananas, sliced	⅛	teaspoon salt
4	tablespoons sugar	¼	teaspoon vanilla extract

Mix pudding according to directions on box using egg yolks mixed with milk. Arrange wafers, sliced bananas and pudding in layers in a 2 quart casserole dish ending with layer of pudding on top; makes 3 layers. Beat egg whites and salt until frothy. Add 1 tablespoon of sugar at a time and beat until meringue is stiff. Spread meringue gently over top. Bake at 375 degrees for 15 minutes. Serves 8.

For another quick version of this recipe, use pudding as directed on box. Do not bake, put layers of whipped cream and top with same.

"The Book" Gift Shop

EMMA'S BANANA PUDDING DELIGHT

(From the oven of Paula Kelly Rogers, daughter of Emma Kelly)

1   small box instant vanilla pudding
1   can of Eagle Brand condensed milk
1   cup milk
1   12 ounce tub Cool Whip
1   8 ounce carton of sour cream (yes, sour cream)
     Vanilla Wafers
     Bananas

Mix pudding, condensed milk and mix well with electric mixer for 2 minutes. Set in refrigerator for 10 minutes to thicken. Mix Cool Whip and sour cream; fold into pudding mixture with spoon and mix well. Layer deep dish with vanilla wafers and bananas. Pour one-third of mixture over bananas. Repeat twice or until pudding is gone. Crumble vanilla wafers and scatter over top for garnish. You could also drizzle chocolate syrup on top. Serves 10 or more.

BETH'S COCONUT PUFFS

(From the kitchen of Beth Sullivan, Crystal River, Florida)

1   cup sweetened condensed milk
3   cups coconut
1   cup chocolate chips
½   cup nuts
1   teaspoon vanilla

Mix all ingredients in a bowl; drop with teaspoon on a greased cookie sheet. Bake at 350 degrees for 8 to 10 minutes.

Trivia: Who was the connection between Emma Kelly and Johnny Mercer and how did they meet? (#19)

LISA'S KOOGLE
(Purchased by marriage, a Yankee Recipe.
We love our daughter-in-law.)

4	eggs
1	cup sugar
1	pound cooked wide noodles
1	pound cottage cheese
1	pint sour cream
1	teaspoon vanilla
½	pound melted margarine
1	jar apple pie filing
½	cup raisin
	Cinnamon to color

Beat together eggs and sugar. Add remaining ingredients. Mix well. Pour into greased pan and bake at 350 degrees for 1 hour. Should be light brown on top.

Note: Also great to serve with a Brunch menu. In the North this is a side dish; here in the South we use it as a dessert, but try it with a Brunch menu. I think I like it that way best, Deb

* Peach filing may be substituted for apple.

Even when a marriage is made in heaven, the
maintenance work has to be done here on earth.

PEACH AND RHUBARB PIE
(From the kitchen of Louise Streed)

Basic two prepared pie crusts (I use the rolled up kind)

- **1 ¼ cups sugar**
- **6 tablespoons all-purpose flour**
- **3 ½ cups peeled and sliced peaches**
- **1 cup sliced rhubarb (thawed frozen or fresh sliced)**
- **1 tablespoon butter**

Preheat oven to 425 degrees. Line a pie pan with one leaf of pie crust. Mix the sugar and flour in a large bowl, add the peaches and rhubarb, tossing well to coat. Pile the fruit into the crust lined pie pan. Dot the butter on top of the fruit. Trim the bottom crust to the edge of the pie pan and wet the edges, place the top crust over the pie and press to the bottom crust. Crimp or flute the edges, cut vents in the top crust.

Bake for 10 minutes and then reduce the oven temperature to 350 degrees and bake from 30 to 40 minutes until crust is browned.

Note: Louise Streed is a local artist and author and she has been with "The Book" Gift Shop for over 10 years. Her beautiful water color of Savannah mansions and scenery are portrayed in her book *Savannah, Her History as seen by an Artist*, and it is one the top sellers in "The Book" Gift Shop. She is one of the artists featured in this cookbook. Look for her work and call "The Book" Gift Shop to place an order.

Trivia: What made it unusual for Mr. Glover to walk Patrick? (#48)

KEY LIME MARGARITA PIE

1 ¼   cups pretzels, crushed
6   tablespoons butter or margarine, melted
½   cup lime juice
1   8 ounce tub Cool whip
¼   cup sugar
1   14 ounce can sweetened condensed milk
1   package unsweetened lemon-lime drink mix

In a large plastic baggie crush whole pretzels. Mix crushed pretzels, sugar and butter. Press firmly into bottom of 9-inch pie tin. Refrigerate until ready to fill.

Using a large bowl; combine milk, lime juice and drink mix powder until well blended. Gently stir in Cool whip topping. Pour into crust.

Set in freezer overnight or if started early enough in the day it should be ready in the late afternoon (between 6 to 7 hours). Before ready to serve, set out for 10 to 15 minutes or until pie cuts easily. Store leftover pie in freezer.

Trivia: What was the subject of the CBS made-for-TV movie that was being filmed at the beginning of "The Book?" (#29)

MIMI'S ICE BOX LEMON PIE

2   medium egg yolks
1   can sweetened condensed milk
6-7   tablespoons fresh lemon juice
1   9 inch graham cracker pie shell

Beat egg yolks (save egg whites for meringue; see below); add milk and lemon juice. Mix well and pour into graham cracker pie crust.

MERINGUE

2   egg whites
½   teaspoon cream of tartar
6   tablespoons sugar

In mixing bowl, beat egg whites adding cream of tartar until it begins to form peaks; adding sugar gradually and continue beating until froth forms. Spread over pie and place in a 350 degree preheated oven for 10-12 minutes or until meringue is golden brown.

Fun Fact: Helen Salter is the name of the Tour Guide who toured Jackie Kennedy Onassis around Savannah. Her granddaughter owns "The Book" Gift Shop.

BILL BILL'S BANANA CREAM PIE

*(In memory of Deborah's grandfather William Salter,
lovingly known as Bill Bill. Two of his favorite desserts were
Banana Cream Pie and Strawberry Shortcake)*

2	small packages cream cheese	1	can condensed milk
1	teaspoon vanilla extract	3	lemons, juiced
	Bananas	1	9 inch graham cracker pie shell

In a mixing bowl, add cream cheese, vanilla, milk and lemon juice and
blend until creamy. Slice bananas and line graham cracker pie shell.
Pour mixture over pie shell carefully, refrigerate and serve chilled.

MS. EMMA'S FAVORITE EGG NOG

*(From the kitchen of Paula Kelly Rogers,
daughter of Emma Kelly)*

4	eggs
1	cup sugar
1	cup dark rum
1	12 ounce light Cool Whip
1	quart soften vanilla ice cream
3	quarts milk

With a mixer beat eggs and sugar until frothy. Blend in rum,
Cool Whip, ice cream and milk. Chill, sprinkle with nutmeg
and serve.

Note: I always wondered what kept Ms. Emma going so long
around the holidays…now I know.

Pamela Lee

Forsyth Park
Savannah Georgia

PAULA'S COFFEE PUNCH
(From the kitchen of Paula Kelly Rogers)

3	quarts strong cold coffee
2	tablespoons vanilla flavoring
2	quarts milk
2	cups sugar

Mix together and pour over 1 gallon of vanilla ice cream.

Trivia: Who was the connection between Emma Kelly and Johnny Mercer and they met by way of what nineteenth century invention? (#19)

SOUTHERN SWEET TEA

2   family size tea bags or 6 small
1   cup sugar (more if you really like sweet)

Place tea bags in a small pot of water; bring to a boil, remove from heat and allow to sit for 15 minutes. Drain into a pitcher being careful not to allow tea bags or tea leaves to enter. Add sugar and enough tap water to make two quarts, stirring constantly. Pour into iced tea glasses and serve with lemon wedge. Allow fresh-brewed tea to sit at room temperature for at least 1 hour before refrigerating.

    Note: Less sugar or more sugar to taste.

SAVANNAH SUMMER TEA

½   Southern sweet tea recipe (from above)
½   fresh lemonade (your favorite recipe)

Mix together and serve in iced tea glasses. Serve with lemon wedge.

Fun Fact: A 'Mural' of Bonaventure Cemetery is painted on one of the walls in "The Book" Gift Shop featuring "The Birdgirl" and also Conrad Aiken's Bench. Come by and see for yourself.

THE GUCCI CARPET BAGGERS FROM OFF

Harbour View © 2003 Sharon Saseen

These are a compilation of recipes from the friends and patrons of "The Book" Gift Shop.

PUMPKIN CORNBREAD MUFFINS
(From the kitchen of Michelle Watson
Dobson, North Carolina)

1 ½	cups cornmeal	1	egg
½	cups self-rising flour	3	tablespoons vegetable oil
1	tablespoon baking powder	¾	cup pumpkin puree
3	tablespoons granulated sugar	1 ½	cups whole milk
1	teaspoon cinnamon		
1	teaspoon salt		

Sift dry ingredients. Beat egg. Stir egg, oil, pumpkin and milk into dry ingredients,(you will have a few lumps).

Pour into greased muffin pan. Bake at 375 degrees for 20 minutes.

Wonderful southern favorite.

GEORGIA BROWN'S BAKED BEANS
(From the oven of Denise Kirkpatrick
Huntsville, Alabama)

4	strips of bacon	½	cup of barbecue sauce
½	red bell pepper, diced	¼	cup brown sugar
1	medium onion, chopped	1	tablespoon of your
2	24 ounce cans of baked beans		favorite BBQ rub
1	can peach pie filing		

In a large skillet, cook bacon until crisp; transfer to a paper towel-lined plate to drain, reserving fat in skillet. Add the bell pepper and onion to the skillet and cook until softened, about 6 minutes. Transfer to baking dish and add beans, barbecue sauce, brown sugar, seasoning, pie filing and crumbled bacon. Mix until combined. Bake uncovered until bubbly; about 45 minutes in a preheated 350 degree oven.

Denise is part of a BBQ cook-off team from the Huntsville, Alabama area. She has competed for some time.

GUCCI CARPET BAG STEAK

(From the kitchen of Margaret Debolt)

3	24 ounce strip steaks
24	small oysters
	Salt and pepper

Slice steaks horizontally with a very sharp knife to within 1-inch of the fat side; stuff with raw oysters and season. Secure with wooden picks. Broil 8 minutes on each side. Slice slantwise, and serve with Maitre D'Hotel Butter (see below).

MAITRE D'HOTEL BUTTER

(From the kitchen of Margaret Debolt & Marcel Carles)

¼	pound (1 stick) butter, melted over very low heat
	Juice of one lemon (about 2 tablespoons)
2	tablespoons chopped parsley
	Salt and pepper

Blend ingredients and serve warm over steaks.

CLAM PIE

(From the oven of Lynn Paska
Schenectady, New York)

This is a treasured recipe from Lynn's Aunt Jennie. As you can tell from the directions, it is a very old recipe and has been handed down for several generations.

3 dozen large chowder clams (to get the juice); strain juice
For every cup of juice, add ½ cup water.
Taste; if too salty, add more water "to taste."
Thicken this to make a gravy, adding a large chunk of butter (approximately 2 tablespoons); set aside
Make biscuit dough of at least 3 cups flour.

Line side of pan (8" diameter x 5" depth) half-way down with dough. Roll out remainder for top.

Remove clams from their shells. Put in gravy and shelled clams, and cover with biscuit dough. Put slits in top for steam to escape.

Bake in very hot oven (450 degrees) until dough rises, then reduce heat to 325 degrees

Bake 40-45 minutes longer.

This recipe is well over 100 years old and has been handed down over the generations in Lynn's family. We thank her for sharing this with us.

SHELLIE'S FROGMORE STEW
(From the kitchen of Shellie Phillips
Baltimore, Maryland)

My husband James and I were married in Savannah, Georgia where we fell in love with the atmosphere, the food, the history and the people. The one dish that always reminds me of Savannah is Low Country Boil or Frogmore Stew. I developed my own recipe for it. Every year on our anniversary, my husband and I sit down with a few close friends and I serve my version of this Southern Treasure.

3	quarts of water
2	cans of beer
½	cup Old Bay Seasoning
4	pounds small red potatoes
4	pounds Hillshire Farms Polish Kielbasa, cut into 1-1/2 inch pieces
8	ears fresh corn, halved
1	extra large onion, sliced thin
4	pounds unpeeled, large fresh shrimp
2	sticks butter
	Old Bay Seasoning
	Cocktail Sauce

Makes 12 servings Prep: 10 Minutes Cook: 30 Minutes

Bring water and beer and ½ cup Old Bay to a rolling boil in a large covered stockpot. Add potatoes; return to a boil, and cook, uncovered 10 minutes. Add sausage, corn and onions, and 1 stick of butter. Return to a boil. Cook 10 minutes or until potatoes are tender. Add shrimp to stockpot; cook 3 to 4 minutes or until shrimp turn pink. Drain. Return drained food to stockpot; add 1 stick of butter. Cover and allow butter to melt. Serve with Old Bay Seasoning and Cocktail Sauce.

The Hillshire Kielbasa adds plenty of richness to this dish so butter may be omitted. However, as a rule use ½ pound of butter for every six people.

Note: Serve on heavy brown paper or newspaper for ease of cleanup.

APPLE FRITTERS
*(From the oven of Lynn Paska
Schenectady, New York)*

This was a favorite recipe of Lynn's mother, Evelyn, who got it from her mother, Johanna. It was "my comfort food," states Lynn. "Oh, how I looked forward to the fall when apple season was in full bloom!"

2	cups flour	3	level teaspoons baking powder
4	teaspoons sugar		
1	cup milk	1	teaspoon vanilla
3	large apples, peeled and sliced		

Mix all ingredients in large bowl. Drop by spoonfuls into hot oil in frying pan. When thoroughly browned on one side, turn over and cook until thoroughly browned on other side. Drain on paper towels. Let cool; serve immediately.

This recipe is well over 100 years old and has been handed down over the generations in Lynn's family. We thank her for sharing this with us.

MY MOTHER'S PEACH COBBLER
(From the kitchen of Shellie Phillips
Baltimore, Maryland)

My mother Helen Gross, while not from Georgia, was a Southern Lady from the foothills of the Virginia Blue Ridge Mountains. She was the casserole queen (a product of her era), but when it came to desserts, her southern roots always took over.

1	tablespoon cornstarch	3	cups sugared,
¼	cup brown sugar		sliced fresh peaches
½	cup cold water	1	tablespoon butter
1	tablespoon lemon juice		

COBBLER CRUST:

1	cup sifted flour	¼	cup soft butter
½	cup sugar	2	tablespoons sugar
1½	teaspoons baking powder	¼	teaspoon nutmeg
½	teaspoon salt	1	teaspoon cinnamon
½	cup milk		

Mix first 3 ingredients; add fruit. Cook and stir until mixture thickens. Add butter and lemon juice. Pour into 8 ¼ x 1 ¾-inch round ovenware cake dish.

Cobbler Crust:

Sift together flour, ½ cup sugar, baking powder, and salt. Add milk and butter all at once; beat smooth. Pour over fruit. Mix 2 tablespoons sugar, nutmeg and cinnamon. Sprinkle over batter. Bake in moderate oven (350 degrees) 30 minutes or until done. Serve warm with cream.

   Note: or use canned or frozen fruits. Drain; use ½ cup syrup instead of water.

   6 servings.

L. Steed

The Gucci Carpet Baggers

BANANA SPLIT CAKE

(From the kitchen of Shellie Phillips
Baltimore, Maryland)

This is a delicious pound cake. It is good with or without the Strawberry Sauce and whipped cream. Try it and I am sure you will agree.

3	cups all-purpose flour		4	eggs
2	teaspoons baking powder		1	medium banana, mashed
1	teaspoon salt		½	cup dairy sour cream
¼	teaspoon baking soda		½	cup milk
1	cup butter or margarine		½	cup instant cocoa mix
1½	cups sugar			Whipped topping
1	teaspoon vanilla extract			

Preheat oven to 350 degrees. Grease and lightly flour a 10-inch tube or bundt pan and set aside. In mixer bowl, beat butter or margarine on medium speed of electric mixer about 30 seconds. Add sugar and vanilla and beat until fluffy. Add eggs, one at a time, beating 1 minute after each addition. Combine banana, sour cream and milk. Add flour mixture to banana mixture, beating well.

Remove 1 cup batter and fold in cocoa mix. Stir until well combined.

Spoon plain batter into prepared pan. Spoon cocoa batter on top in a ring, do not spread to edges.

Bake in preheated oven for 60 to 70 minutes, or until cake tests done. Cool for 10 minutes on rack, remove from pan, place back on rack and cool completely.

Serve with Strawberry Sauce

STRAWBERRY SAUCE

4   cups fresh or frozen whole unsweetened
       strawberries
1   cup water
¾   cup sugar
2   tablespoons cornstarch

Crush 1 cup of berries and add 1 cup water. Cook for 2 minutes, drain and crush. Combine sugar and cornstarch. Stir into crushed strawberry mixture. Cook and stir until mixture becomes bubbly, then cook for 2 minutes longer. Halve remaining 3 cups strawberries and stir into sauce. Chill.

Serve each slice with Strawberry Sauce and top with whipped topping.

THE SOUTHERN HOLIDAY

Hall Street Christmas © Sharon Saseen

SAVANNAH STYLE

TRADITIONAL HOLIDAY MENU

At least from our kitchen at holiday time

Glazed Ham

Giblet Gravy

Carrots And Onions

Deep Fried Turkey

Macaroni And Cheese

Sweet Potato Casserole

Cranberry Crescent Rolls

Christmas Peppermint Pie

Broccoli And Rice Casserole

Country Cornbread Dressing

Holiday Cookies

HOLIDAY MIMOSA

1   bottle of champagne or sparkling wine
1   cup orange juice (fresh is best)
½   cup of cranberry juice

In a large pitcher mix ingredients, add ice and serve chilled. Garnish with orange slices or cherries.

Note: Nice to serve with your Holiday Brunch.

BRUNCH CASSEROLE

1 ½ pounds sausage *
1   cup sharp Cheddar cheese
6   eggs
     Butter

6   pieces bread (French loaf works well)
2   cups milk **
     Salt & pepper to taste

Brown sausage in saucepan, drain off fat. If using loaf, slice bread to ½-inch to 1-inch thick; butter both sides and lay in a casserole dish; put aside. In a mixing bowl beat eggs, stir in milk , cheese, salt and pepper; blend well. Pour mixture over bread slices, crumble sausage over mixture; cover. Must sit 5-6 hours before baking. Bake at 350 degrees for 45 minutes.

Note: This is very easy to fix the night before; just pop it in the oven the next morning. Cut up some fresh fruit and serve with yogurt and homemade granola. Serve mimosas and coffee. Your holiday guest will adore you and think you can do it all, even during the hustle-bustle of the holidays.

* You can use mild or spicy sausage (I mix both together).
**whole, skim or even half & half

Our Little Fun Time:

Instead of purchasing big expensive gifts for the whole family we have had a lot of fun purchasing unique fun smaller gifts for everyone over the last few years. On Christmas eve or Christmas day, we each sneak around and pop our little fun gifts into the stockings that we each hang on the inside staircase.

Each stocking has its on name tag, of course. After dinner we one-by-one go through our stockings to see what's in store. We look forward to this fun time together.

AUNT BETH'S FAVORITE BREAKFAST
(From the kitchen of Beth Sullivan, sister–in–law
Crystal River, Florida)

WAFFLES WITH STEWED APPLES, TOPPED WITH ICE CREAM

3	cups milk	2	teaspoons vanilla extract
3	eggs, beaten	3	cups all-purpose flour
8	tablespoons melted margarine	3	teaspoons baking powder
3	tablespoons sugar		

Blend milk and eggs together, add melted margarine and sugar; stir in vanilla. Combine dry ingredients and add milk mixture. Use a whisk to fluff up. Heat waffle iron and spray cooking oil. Pour enough batter to fill the waffle iron; close and bake until steaming stops and waffles are crisp and golden.

Prepare stewed apples before you cook the waffles. Combine 1 cup brown sugar, 1 tablespoon cornstarch, ½ teaspoon cinnamon, ½ cup water and 2 tablespoons margarine in a saucepan with 5-6 pared and sliced apples. Cook and stir over medium heat, about 5 to 8 minutes until tender.

Place waffles on a plate, top with 1 scoop of vanilla ice cream and add stewed apples.

Note: Even if you use a pre-mix pancake mix and an apple pie filling, make sure you add the cinnamon to the apples.

This is so much fun to serve; who has ice cream for breakfast? This is the champion of Breakfast.

Every year, during the holidays, Beth and her husband, my brother, Richard, fix this for breakfast. It is truly a tradition with us and who doesn't want to have ice cream for breakfast.

Fun Fact: John Lee Hancock was the screenplay writer for "The Movie" and filming took place in Savannah the summer of 1997.

DADDY JOE'S FROZEN WAFFLE BREAKFAST
(From the kitchen of Joe Sullivan, my dad)

Go to the store, buy your favorite frozen waffles and place in toaster, as per instructions on box. Serve hot with syrup, coffee, milk or orange juice.

Personal Note: You can laugh, but my dad has come a long way to learning how to make the toaster work. A couple of years ago he called us asking if there was a recipe for boiling water so that he could make instant coffee, no kidding! Thanks for your contribution, Pop! (it is better to keep him out of the kitchen)

FRENCH TOAST SANDWICHES

16	slices bread (white is best)	3	large eggs
1	8 ounce package cream cheese		Dash nutmeg
½	cup pecans, chopped	¼	teaspoon cinnamon
2	teaspoons vanilla butter-nut	¼	stick butter
1	cup half and half	2	tablespoons oil

Remove crust from bread. In a mixing bowl combine cream cheese, pecans, and 1 teaspoon of vanilla butter-nut flavoring. Spread this mixture on 8 slices of bread then top with other slices. In a large bowl (large enough to dip sandwich in), mix half & half, eggs, nutmeg, cinnamon and 1 teaspoon of vanilla butter-nut. Melt butter and 2 tablespoons oil in a griddle at 350 degrees. Immerse sandwiches in egg mixture, covering completely; place onto griddle and cook until golden brown on both sides. Dust with powered sugar, if desired.

Trivia: What is Luther Driggers real name? (#26)

DEBORAH'S MONKEY BREAD

1	cup pecans or walnuts, chopped finely	2	cans buttermilk biscuits
1	stick butter	½	cup light brown sugar
1	tablespoon cinnamon	½	cup sugar

Grease a bundt pan and line bottom with nuts. In a small saucepan melt butter. In a small bowl, mix cinnamon and sugars together. Pull biscuits apart, quarter, dip into butter then into sugars; place in pan. After placing all the biscuits in pan sprinkle with sugars (you may need a little more mixture); cook at 350 degrees for 30 to 35 minutes. Place in dish, pull apart and enjoy!

Note: These are a favorite with our family during the holiday season. Deborah usually serves them as a **breakfast appetizer.**

SAVANNAH CINNAMON FRENCH TOAST

1	tablespoon cinnamon mix*	2	eggs

Beat eggs; add Savannah cinnamon mix, then dip bread slices into mixture. Fry as usual.

OPTIONAL RECIPE
Use Savannah praline mix* instead of cinnamon mix.

* Savannah Cinnamon mix and Praline mix may be purchased from "The Book" Gift Shop

CRANBERRY CRESCENT ROLLS
(From Deb's kitchen)

2	cans crescent rolls	½	can whole cranberries

Roll out crescent dough, place ½ to 1 teaspoon cranberries on top; roll into triangle, cook according to directions on can. Brush with butter and serve hot.

PRALINE/HAZELNUT BUTTER

2	tablespoons praline mix*	1	stick butter, softened

Mix together and use as a spread on toast, pancakes, bagels, waffles, etc.

Note: This also makes a nice gift. Put it with a pancake mix in a nice gift basket, a big holiday bow, and you have a great teacher's gift.

* Savannah Praline mix may be purchased from "The Book" Gift Shop.

MEMA'S HOT CHEESE DIP
(*Shane's mom*)

I think just about every family has a mema and I'm glad this one's mine

1	cup chopped onion	1	cup grated sharp
1	cup Hellmann's mayonnaise		Cheddar cheese

Put in small casserole dish and bake at 350 degrees until bubbly. Serve hot with crackers.

Note: I absolutely love this anytime, but it is always special to me around the holidays; time with family!

Come join us in Savannah for the holiday. Our annual downtown Holiday Tour of Homes is not to be missed.

PRALINE NUTCRACKER

12	whole graham crackers	1	cup pecans, chopped
¾	cup butter	½	cup sugar
½	cup praline mix *	½	teaspoon baking soda

Preheat oven to 275 degrees. Line a 12 x 17-inch baking pan with parchment paper. Break graham crackers along lines to get 48 pieces. Tightly arrange crackers in bottom of the pan. Sprinkle with pecans. In a saucepan combine butter and sugar. Gently boil for 3 to 4 minutes. Stir in praline mix and heat just until boiling. Stir in baking soda. Pour over crackers and bake at 275 degrees for 20 minutes. Cool and remove from pan into cookie container.

* Savannah Praline mix may be purchased from "The Book" Gift Shop.

PRALINE PARTY MIX

6	cups Chex Mix	2	cups pecan halves
¼	cup butter	½	cup brown sugar
⅓	cup praline mix*	½	teaspoon baking soda

In a 13 x 9-inch pan mix together Chex mix and pecan halves. In a saucepan melt butter, brown sugar and praline mix; heat until boiling. Gently cook for 2 minutes. Remove from heat and stir in baking soda until foamy. Pour mixture over Chex mix and pecans coating well. Bake at 250 degrees for 1 hour stirring once during baking. Spread onto cookie sheet to cool.

*Savannah Praline mix may be purchased from "The Book" Gift Shop.

Fun Fact: Moe Fetze was Lou Driggers real name.

RED HOT SALAD
*(From the kitchen of Deborah's cousin
Cristina Dimick, Beaverton, Oregon)*

2	cups water	16	ounce package jello
½	cup red hots candy		(lemon or lime)
2	cups applesauce		
	Cool Whip		

In a pot, boil 2 cups water; add red hots and stir until melted, add jello and applesauce, stirring well. Pour into jello mold, let stand until firm. Place lettuce leaves on plate, invert jello mold on top. Place whipcream in center.

Note: This makes a beautiful presentation and is a favorite of all kids.

SULLIVAN'S MACARONI & CHEESE
*(This is a Sullivan family favorite that is
always made at our gatherings)*

1	box elbow macaroni	1	block Cheddar cheese,
5	eggs		grated
1	cup milk		Salt and pepper to taste
	Butter		

Boil noodles as per directions on box (I usually undercook then just a little, about 1 minute less than suggested time). Let it cool slightly. In another bowl beat eggs and milk together. Pour just a teaspoon into the bottom of a casserole dish; then layer ingredients starting with noodles, then cheese, then pour some of the egg & milk mixture.

I salt a little and pepper a lot on top of the egg & milk mixture for my family's taste. Continue layering ending up with a layer of cheese and mixture on top. Add a few pats of butter on top and bake at 350 degrees for 45 minutes (may take a little longer), you do not want the macaroni & cheese overcooked, but also you do not want it too runny either. Allow the topping to brown-up.

PRALINE CARROTS AND ONIONS

½	stick butter	1	bag frozen sliced carrots
2	Vidalia onions, sliced,	¼	cup brown sugar
	separated into rings	⅓	cup Praline mix *

In a frying pan melt butter; add carrots, onions and brown sugar. Cook on medium heat until tender. Add praline mix and cook for 5 minutes. Serve hot.

* Praline mix may be purchased from "The Book" Gift Shop.

SOUTHERN PRALINE YAMS

1	40 ounce can yams, drainedchunks,	1	20 ounce can pineapple drained
½	cup praline mix *	½	cup brown sugar
2	tablespoons butter		

In a baking dish combine yams and pineapple; dot with butter. Combine praline mix and brown sugar; pour over top of yams and pineapple. If desired, sprinkle pecans on top. Bake at 350 degrees for 20 to 30 minutes. (Savannah Cinnamon mix * may be substituted for the Savannah Praline mix).

* Both the Savannah Praline mix and Cinnamon mix may be purchased from "The Book" Gift Shop.

SWEET POTATO CASSEROLE

1	cup milk	1	cup sugar
2	eggs	3	cups sweet potatoes, mashed
2	tablespoons vanilla butter-nut	1 ½	sticks butter or margarine
½	teaspoon cinnamon		
¼	cup orange juice		

In a mixing bowl, combine all ingredients and beat well. Pour into a buttered 13x9x2-inch casserole dish; set aside while making topping (see below).

TOPPING

1	cup light brown sugar	1	cup pecans, chopped
⅓	cup self-rising flour	⅓	cup butter or margarine, melted

Combine all ingredients, blending together well. Pour over casserole and bake at 350 degrees for 35 minutes.

CHRISTMAS JAM

| 12 | ounces fresh cranberries | 4 | cups sugar |
| 2 | 10 ounce packages frozen strawberries, thawed | 1 | 3 ounce bottle liquid pectin |

Chop cranberries in food processor or blender until berries are coarsely chopped. Combine cranberries, strawberries, and sugar in a large, heavy pot. Bring to a boil; boil 1 minute, stirring occasionally. Remove from heat, add pectin, and bring back to a boil. Boil 1 minute, stirring constantly. Remove from heat and skim off foam. Quickly pour into hot sterilized jars. Leave ¼-inch air space. Wipe jar rims and cover with metal lids. Place in a large pot, cover with boiling water. Return to a boil for 5 minutes.

Note: Very nice for the holiday or as hostess gifts.

BROCCOLI-RICE CASSEROLE
(From the kitchen of Don Dimick, Deborah's Father Minister of Music, Ardsley Park Baptist Church, Savannah, Georgia)

2	10 ounce packages frozen chopped broccoli, thawed
¾	cup chopped celery
¾	cup chopped onion
½	cup margarine
2	10 ounce cans cream of chicken soup
2	cups uncooked minute rice
1	cup shredded Cheddar cheese
1	cup sliced water chestnuts

Combine in large bowl all ingredients, mixing together well. Pour into greased baking dish and bake at 300 degrees for 1 hour. Makes 6 to 8 servings.

Topping (Optional)

    1   sleeve crushed Ritz crackers (more if you like)
    2   tablespoons butter, melted

Add topping to casserole during the last 15 minutes of cooking.
Note: I highly recommend the topping, it's very good.

Sullivan's Holiday Corn Casserole

1 can whole-kernel corn, drained	18 ounce package Jiffy corn muffin mix
1 can cream-style corn	1 cup sour cream
1 stick butter, melted	1 tablespoon mayonnaise

In a large bowl, mix together all ingredients and pour into a greased casserole dish. Bake at 350 degrees for 45 to 60 minutes or until golden brown.
Serves 6 to 8.

Trivia: Why did a certain employer call his employee Jack the one-eyed Jill? (#75)

COUNTRY CORNBREAD DRESSING
(From the kitchen of Deborah's mom Nancy Dimick)

Cornbread for 16 servings (prepared)
5   slices of white bread
2 ½   cups of finely chopped green peppers
2 ½   cups of finely chopped celery
2 ½   cups of finely chopped onions
5   cups liquid from cooked giblets
1   cup liquid from turkey drippings
6   eggs, beaten
    Salt and pepper to taste (although it needs very little)

Preheat oven to 350 degrees.

Crumble cornbread into a large bowl. Tear white bread into small pieces and add to cornbread. Add peppers, celery, and onions. Stir in all liquids until ingredients are thoroughly mixed. Add eggs and mix well; add salt and pepper.

Set aside 3 to 5 cups of the mixture to add to Giblet Gravy (see recipe). Pour the remaining mixture into a 9x13x2-inch dish (3 quarts). Place in preheated oven and bake approximately 1 ½ hours or until well done and lightly browned on top. Serves 18 to 20 people.

Note: This recipe was passed down from Nancy's Grandmother Sheppard and is almost 100 years old. As you can tell it serves quite a few people, but with our group, it is just enough. This is the best homemade cornbread and giblet gravy recipes we have had the pleasure in eating. Since Deborah was raised on this, she is a little biased.

COUNTRY GIBLET GRAVY

(From the kitchen of Grandma Sheppard,
Deb's Great Grandmother)

Cooked giblets from turkey, cut up
7   **cups liquid from cooked giblets**
3 - 5 **cups uncooked cornbread dressing mixture**
3   **eggs, boiled and cut up**
    Salt and pepper to taste

Cook the thoroughly rinsed giblets in a 5 quart pot for 1 ½ hours, adding water when needed to keep the pot filled. Remove giblets from the liquid; drain giblets. Remove meat from neck bone, cut up other giblets; set aside. Measure enough liquid for at least 7 cups; put liquid back into the 5 quart pot and return giblets to liquid. Add 3 to 5 cups of uncooked dressing mixture (depending on how thick you want your gravy). Add boiled egg pieces. Cook on moderately low heat for 1 hour, or a little longer, if necessary, stirring often to keep gravy from sticking to pot.
Salt and pepper to taste

Note: This gravy is delicious on cornbread dressing (see recipe), rice and turkey.

People who brag about their ancestors are like
carrots – the best part of them is underground.

DEEP FRIED TURKEY
(From the deep fryer of Shane Sullivan)

2	gallons peanut oil
1	can Cajun spice
1	10-12 pounds frozen turkey
2	cans beer (optional)

This should only be cooked outdoors in a deep fryer.

Allow turkey to thaw in refrigerator. The day before cooking, wash bird thoroughly. Do not dry. Place turkey in aluminum foil and season with as much as you like (I use The Lady and Sons silly salt and house seasoning *), rubbing all over. Wrap tightly and place turkey in refrigerator until ready to cook. Pour oil into 16 quart deep fryer and heat to 350 degrees. Remove foil and place turkey into basket, pour 1 can of beer (if using) into pot then carefully lower into hot oil. As turkey is boiling, about 25 minutes add second can of beer. Turkey should reach a beautiful golden brown, about 45-50 minutes total cooking time.

Note: If you've always wanted to try a fried turkey, this is it. Also, if you're dieting, use Lite Beer, Right!

Caution: Do not over indulge yourself with the Julia Childs' syndrome: *a little beer for the bird and a little more beer for me.*

* The Lady & Sons silly salt and house seasoning may be purchased from "The Book" Gift Shop.

Fun Fact: Helen Driscol was Serena Dawes' real name.

GLAZED HAM

1	ham, cooked per directions
½	cup cinnamon mix *
½	cup brown sugar
½	cup pineapple or orange juice

Mix together all ingredients and use as a basting sauce for ham.

OPTIONAL RECIPE

| ½ | cup cinnamon mix * | 1 | 8 ounce coke |

Mix together for basting sauce.

* Savannah Cinnamon mix may be purchased from "The Book" Gift Shop.

PRALINE DIP

18	ounce cream cheese, softened
½	cup pecans, finely chopped
¼	cup Praline mix *

Mix all ingredients together until smooth. Serve with slices of red and green apples or butter cookies*. To keep apple slices from turning, sprinkle with lemon juice.

* Praline mix and butter cookies may be purchased from "The Book" Gift Shop.

Pam Lee

STEPH'S BOURBON BALLS

(Contributed by our daughter Stephanie Sullivan Atlanta, Georgia)

1	cup pound cake, cut into cubes
½	cup toasted pecans
½	cup confectioners' sugar
2	tablespoons bourbon (a little more if you like it stronger)
	Cocoa to coat

If you cannot find toasted pecans, place halves on cookie sheet and bake at 350 degrees for just a couple of minutes, but watch to make sure they do not burn. In a mixing bowl, crumble cake, add pecans and sugar making sure all is blended together well and fine. Add a little bourbon at a time to moisten so as to make dough. Pour out onto a lightly dusted wax paper of confectioners' sugar. Pull off enough to form a ½ to ¾-inch ball, roll in cocoa and enjoy.

Note: You could use a food processor to blend ingredients; then add bourbon. These are great around the holidays, but make enough for everyone and if you're like us, keep your eye on Stephanie because she will pull a Joe Odom and add more bourbon.

MEMA'S HOLIDAY COOKIES
KOURABIEDES
Greek Cookie
(From the kitchen of Helen Sullivan, Savannah, Georgia)

1	pound sweet butter	1	teaspoon vanilla
½	cup powered sugar	½	teaspoon almond extract
1	egg yolk (optional)	6	tablespoons toasted
1	jigger whiskey		almonds, chopped finely
4	cups sifted flour		(optional; but not as
	Confectioners' sugar		good without these)

Beat butter and sugar until creamy, about 15 minutes; add egg yolk, flavorings and almonds, beating until well blended. Take beater out and gradually add sifted flour to make soft dough. Add more flour if needed (about ¼ cup). Mold into small crescent shapes (3-4 inch size) and place onto baking sheet, about 1-inch apart; bake at 350 degrees for 20 minutes, or just until very lightly browned. Allow to cool slightly and roll in confectioners' sugar. Makes about 5 dozen.

Note: This is a family tradition; "The girls" of the family make a cookie baking date, we meet one weekend and bake up a storm. Then we have dozens of cookies to share with family and friends.

WHITE CHOCOLATE CHERRY ALMOND POUND CAKE
(From the kitchen of Ron & Kay Walker, Pooler, Georgia)

1	18.25 package white cake mix	1	12 ½ ounce can Solo almond filling
⅓	cup oil		
1	cup white chocolate chips	⅓	cup sour cream
4	eggs	1	cup dried cherries
	Powdered sugar		

Preheat oven to 325 degrees. Grease and flour bundt pan. Combine cake mix, sour cream, almond filling, oil, and eggs. Blend on medium speed for 2 minutes. Fold in white chocolate chips and dried cherries. Evenly spread batter into pan. Bake 50 to 60 minutes, until toothpick inserted comes out clean. Cool for 10 minutes. Carefully remove cake from pan and cool completely. Sprinkle with powdered sugar.

CHRISTMAS PEPPERMINT PIE
(From Deb's kitchen)

1	envelope plain gelatin	1-1½ capfuls of peppermint
¼	cup cold waterflavoring	(use cap on bottle)
½	cup whipping cream	1 Oreo cookie crust
1 ½	cups whipping cream, whipped	
8	ounce soft peppermint candy, crushed	

Pour gelatin into water; set aside. In a small saucepan pour ½ cup whipping cream with candy, and ½ capful of peppermint flavoring over low heat until candy melts. Add gelatin, mix well. Let cool and fold in whipped cream. Pour into crust. Chill. Just before serving, add 1 capful of peppermint flavoring to ½ container of cool whip; spread on top of pie and sprinkle top of cool whip with crushed peppermint candy.

Note: Garnish each individual slice with a mini-candy cane.

GINGERBREAD CAKE

(From the kitchen of Margaret Debolt and John Wesley Hotel)

½   cup vegetable shortening
½   cup brown sugar, firmly packed
1   tablespoon grated orange peel
3   eggs
1   cup dark molasses
¾   cup hot water
2   teaspoons dry instant coffee
⅓   cup orange juice
3   cups sifted flour
2   teaspoons ginger
1   teaspoon cinnamon
1   teaspoon baking soda
1   teaspoon baking powder
1   teaspoon salt
1   teaspoon nutmeg
½   cup currants
½   cup finely chopped pecans

Preheat oven to 350 degrees. Cream together shortening, sugar, orange peel, and eggs; blend in molasses, water, coffee, and juice. Sift dry ingredients into batter. Beat until smooth. Stir in currants and pecans. Pour into greased and floured 13 x 9-inch pan. Bake for 40 to 45 minutes. Serve warm or cold, with whipped cream or an orange or lemon sauce.

MOON RIVER COCONUT CREAM PIE

¼   cup flour
¼   teaspoon salt
3   eggs
2   tablespoons butter
1   9 inch pie shell

½   cup sugar
1 ½   cups milk, scalded
1   cup coconut
½   teaspoon vanilla

Mix flour, sugar and salt in top of double boiler; scald milk, then add to mixture; stir well. Cook until thick and smooth, stirring constantly. Beat egg yolks well and add to mixture; cooking about another 2 minutes, stirring constantly. Remove from heat; add butter, coconut and vanilla. Pour mixture into pie shell; set aside.

MERINGUE

3   egg whites
¼   teaspoon cream of tartar

½   cup sugar

Beat egg whites and cream of tartar until it peaks; add in sugar 1 teaspoon at a time, beating constantly until frothy. Spread over pie, baking at 350 degrees or just until meringue browns.

Moon River has always been special, not only because of Johnny Mercer, but Emma Kelly would play this for me as I came into Hannah's East at the Pirate's House. Living on the Southside of Savannah near Isle of Hope, we have a chance to see Moon River all the time.

Trivia: What was written on Conrad Aiken's bench? (#9)

CHRISTMAS PUNCH

1	large can pineapple juice	3	quarts ginger ale
2	48 ounce bottles cranberry juice cocktail	½	cup sugar
		1	ounce almond flavoring

Mix all ingredients together. Refrigerate.
Makes about 40-50 servings.

FAMOUS SAVANNAH CINNAMON HOLIDAY PUNCH

| ½ | gallon apple juice | ½ | cup cinnamon mix * |

Mix together; heat and serve. That's all there is to it, simple.
Draw a crowd of family and friends with this fragrant and delicious
hot mulled punch.

* Savannah Cinnamon mix may be purchased from "The Book" Gift Shop.

CHRISTMAS WATERMELON
(From the kitchen of Margaret Debot and Helen Kehoe Crolly)

A unique Southern tradition When melons are in season, select
a large, firm one. Remove a cone-shaped plug, (about 1 ½-inches
wide at the top). Pour champagne into watermelon. Replace plug
and cover well with melted, cooled paraffin. Store in a cool, dark
place until the holiday season. Chill and serve.

APPLE MARTINI

1   **jigger* vodka**
1   **jigger apple juice**
     Green apple to garnish

1   **jigger sour apple**
     schnapps

Pour jiggers into shaker with ice. Strain and pour into martini glass. Cut slices of apple and garnish.

   Note: For an extra special treat, try some green sour apple hard candy to garnish.

* We use the tall 'Birdgirl' shot glasses which can be purchased from "The Book" Gift Shop, call (912) 233-3867.

SOUR APPLE TINI

2   **parts Vodka**
     Splash extra-dry Vermouth

3   **parts sour apple mix**

Pour ingredients into shaker with ice and pour into martini glasses. Garnish with slice of green apple. Holiday garnish with a cherry and it will look like a Christmas tree.

HOLIDAY MARTINI

3   **ounces Vodka**
2   **teaspoons peppermint schnapps**
2   **ounces club soda**

Pour all ingredients into shaker with ice; shake until cold. Pour into chilled martini glass, garnish with a candy cane or sprinkle crushed candy peppermint on top. Fun and Festive.

Trivia: When did the shooting take place? (#1)

CHOCOLATE COFFEE

| 4 | teaspoons cocoa mix | Cinnamon |
| 1 | teaspoon instant coffee | |

Mix together cocoa and coffee with hot water; add sugar and cream to taste, sprinkle with cinnamon. Great after dinner coffee on a cool night or with Lace Cookies (see recipe) or other desserts.

Note: During the holidays sprinkle with a little cut-up Andes chocolate mint candies and/or some peppermints. Also, try inserting a sucker stick into the small size peppermint patties and use as a stirring stick. **Or,** package this up in cellophane bags with a bow, tag and directions and place in everyone's stockings.

SAVANNAH EGG N.O.G.
(This is great if made up the day before serving)

STEP ONE:

| 12 | egg yolks (keep egg whites for step 2) | 2 | cups Dark Rum, Bandy or Bourbon |
| 1 | pound confectioners' sugar | | |

In a mixing bowl large enough to hold ingredients, beat egg yolks until light and frothy. Gradually beat in confectioner's sugar, ¼ cup at a time. Stirring constantly, add the beverage of your choice. If this is for the same day, let stand for 60 minutes before adding to step two.

Note: Make sure you add just one liquor and not all three, like others we know.

STEP TWO:

| 2-4 | cups of liquor (from step 1) | 2 | quarts whipping cream |
| 8-12 | egg whites | 1 | cup Peach Brandy (optional) |

In a large bowl combine liquor and whipping cream, beating constantly, then peach brandy, if used. Cover; refrigerate for at least three hours. In another bowl beat egg whites until stiff. Fold eggs carefully into mixture. Serve cold. Add a sprinkle of cinnamon or nutmeg to top. Serves 10-12.

BEANIE WEENIES
(From the grill of Dick & Shane)

1	bag charcoal	Mayonnaise
1	container lighter fluid	Mustard
2	cans beer (optional)	Ketchup
4	packages beef hot dogs	Relish
4	packages of hot dog buns	Cheese
	Onions, chopped	

DEB'S SWEET BAKED BEAN CASSEROLE

While preparing charcoal for grill, place hotdogs in dish, pour beer over them allowing them to soak. After grill is hot, place hot dogs on top to cook. (I like mine really burned, but this is not for everyone). After all hot dogs are through cooking or burning, place into a large serving dish. Paper plates are set out, so we do not have to wash additional dishes. Place everything on table allowing everyone to fix their own. We use Deb's Sweet Baked Bean Casserole (see recipe) as a topping, the beanie portion. Usually serving 18-20.

Most of you are probably thinking, is this guy for real? Well, I actually look forward to fixing this meal with my brother-in-law, Dick. We fix this meal during our Christmas vacation, which is spent with most all of the family. Our family each takes a night or day to cook and well, this is our specialty. Dick and I usually have a couple of adult beverages while cooking, which makes it even more fun to fix such a meal. Two grown men, laughing and carrying on while grilling hotdogs; what a sight to see. The fun part about this is that we burn a few too many and therefore, we have to taste test them for quality control. Also, if you burn them and you happen to drop them on the ground no one can really tell the difference, they're all gritty anyway.

Making memories, that's what it's all about. Making memories with your family.

Enjoy!

New Year's Menu

(For us it consist of Hoppin' Johns, Corn Bread and Collard Greens)

Hoppin' Johns

1	pound dried black-eyed peas
2	medium onions, chopped
6	cups cold water
½	pound slab bacon, cutinto 1-inch cubes
1	teaspoon Tabasco sauce
1	teaspoon salt
1	cup raw rice
1 ½	cups boiling water

Wash peas. Place in a large pot with cold water, bring to a boil, boil 2 minutes, cover; remove from heat and let sit 1 hour. Cook bacon slowly until brown on all sides; use tongs to turn bacon; reserve grease. Add bacon, Tabasco, and salt to peas. Bring to a boil, lower heat, and simmer covered for 30 minutes. Sauté onion in bacon grease until translucent. Add onions, grease, rice and boiling water to peas. Cover and simmer, stirring occasionally, for 30 minutes, or until rice is tender. It should be moist, but not wet, and most certainly not dry. Taste for seasoning; you will probably need more salt. Serve with cold stewed tomatoes and/or collard greens (see recipes).

Note: Hoppin' Johns is traditionally eaten in the south on New Year's Day to bring luck in the coming year. You may substitute steak o'lean or fatback for the bacon, but the flavor is not as good.

COLLARD GREENS

(From the kitchen of my sister-in-law,
Beth Sullivan, Crystal River, Florida)

1	bunch fresh turnip greens	3-4	cups water
1	ham hock	1	tablespoon sugar
1	tablespoon hot pepper vinegar	½ -1	teaspoon salt

Strip the center stem from the leaves and wash thoroughly. In a large covered Dutch oven, place 3-4 cups water with ham hock; bring to a boil. Add salt, sugar, greens, and hot pepper vinegar. Cook for 45 minutes on medium heat or until tender. Remove ham hock, cool; cut into pieces. Reserve 2 cups of the liquid. Use 2 large knives and crisscross cut the ham hock. Add the cut ham hock and reserved liquid into the pot, keep warm and add 1 tablespoon margarine or butter. Serve with hot pepper vinegar and hot cornbread.

Note: You can cook turnip greens or mustard greens the same way, except use the roots with the turnips.

Optimism: A cheerful frame of mind that
enables a tea kittle to sing even though
it's in hot water up to its nose

"THE BOOK" EXTRAS

Vines of Wisteria © 2002 Sharon Saseen

"THE BOOK" ATTRACTIONS

TOP "MIDNIGHT" ATTRACTIONS

"The Book" Gift Shop - located on beautiful Calhoun Square and NOGS in the Historic District, we are the 'Headquarters' for all your 'Midnight' needs. Just come in and listen to Emma Kelly playing on CD or watch the A&E special of Midnight in Savannah. After perusing through all the memorabilia and winding your way to the back room you will hear "The Book" on CD being read aloud. Many people have described us a being a 'mini-museum' on steroids because of all of the different products relating to "The Book." You'll find unique and exclusive items for a keepsake or you may find something to take back home to a loved one or a 'Midnight' fan. We are located at 127 E. Gordon Street, Savannah, Georgia 31401.

"The Book" Tour is for anyone who enjoyed "The Book" or "The Movie" and want to know just a little more about "The Characters" and their going-ons. If you are lodging in the Historic District we can arrange pick-up for you or you can contact "The Book" Gift Shop for further details. Also, at certain times of the year both Grayline Tours and Oglethorpe Tours offer a "Book" Tour. For information or to book a tour please contact us at (912) 233-3867.

Mercer House is the last home Jim Williams occupied. It is currently opened for an Architectural Tour and there is No Mention of "The Book" or any happenings that took place in "The House." Days and hours are seasonal. They are located on Monterey Square, one square East of "The Book" Gift Shop, at 429 Bull Street. You may contact them directly at (912) 236-6352.

Mrs. Wilkes' Boarding House is a must for anyone visiting Savannah for the first time or those returning. Located at 107 West Jones Street, the family has owned and operated this boarding house and dining room since the mid 1960's. They are opened daily, Monday-Friday, from 11:00am to 2:00pm. There are no reservations and those lining-up for lunchtime will not be disappointed once allowed inside and seated at the dinner table.

The Telfair Museum is located on Telfair Square at 121 Barnard Street and are opened daily; Sunday & Monday 1:00pm to 5:00pm and Tuesday-

Saturday from 10:00am to 5:00pm. The museum is very beautiful and among its' many exhibits stands the statue of "The Birdgirl," on loan from the Trosdal Family cemetery plot. Since this is a museum there are no photos allowed to be taken inside. For further information you may contact the Telfair at (912) 232-1177.

Bonaventure Cemetery is a must visit for all those trying to pique their curiosity of those who have gone before us. The Old Section of the cemetery is filled with head-stones from prior to the turn-of-the century. This section includes Johnny Mercer, Conrad Aikens, Trosdal family (where the "Birdgirl" statue was located), and the Lawton family, just to name a few.

Club-One is still host to The Lady Chablis. At least once a month Chablis pays a visit to the club as a top performer, of course, as only Chablis will. She is still a hot commodity when visiting Savannah and her show will sell-out quickly. For show times contact Club-One at (912) 232-0200.

The Olde Pink House Restaurant, located at 23 Abercorn Street is fun to visit in the early evening after a busy day of shopping and site-seeing. Downstairs is the Olde Tavern where you can just sit and relax, order appetizers, dinner and drinks or just mellow-out to the sound of the talented pianist Gale Thurmond. For information or reservations contact them at (912) 232-4286.

Clary's Café is another one those places mentioned in "The Book" as having unusual characters show up for breakfast or lunch. Located at Abercorn Street, they are just across Calhoun Square from "The Book" Gift Shop. Whether you get there for breakfast, lunch or just a glass of fresh lemonade, it's worth the stop.

Experience a downtown **Bed & Breakfast** and take lasting memories back home with you. There are so many beautiful Bed & Breakfast's in Savannah and no two are just alike. You cannot go wrong in staying in one of these great mansions. Also, if your travel takes you to Beaufort, South Carolina, make sure you visit the Beaufort Inn. They are listed in the National Registry of Historic Hotels in America and their dining room is second-to-none.

OUR FAVORITE HOUSE MUSEUMS

GREEN-MELDRIM HOUSE
1 West Macon Street
(912) 232-1251
Tuesday, Thursday, Friday – 10:00am to 4:00pm
(last tour 3:30pm)
Saturday – 10:00am to 1:00pm
(last tour 12:30pm)
Adult: $5.00   Child: $3.00

They are usually opened at these times unless there is a church function
If you attend their church service on Sunday morning, visitors are invited
over to the House for refreshments.
Note: This is one of our favorite House Museums.

ANDREW LOW HOUSE
329 Abercorn Street
(912) 233-6854
Monday-Saturday – 10:00am to 4:30pm (last tour 4:00pm)
Sunday – 12:00pm to 4:30pm (last tour 4:00pm)
Closed on Thursdays
Adult: $7.50   Child & Scout: $4.50
Military: Free

DAVENPORT HOUSE
(Haunted)
324 East State Street
(912) 236-8097
Monday-Saturday – 10:00am to 4:30pm (last tour 4:00pm)
Sunday – 1:00pm to 4:30pm (last tour 4:00pm)
Adult: $7.50 Child: $3.50 (AAA discount)

HISTORY OF "THE BIRDGIRL"

The Trosdal Family plot: L-57

This beautiful statue once stood vigil over the Trosdal family plot in the garden of Bonaventure Cemetery. When John Berendt wrote his book he requested Random House publishing to use a local photographer. That artist was Jack Leigh of Savannah and the photograph he took is the legendary "Birdgirl." Jack said that the reason he snapped this photo was because it 'intrigued' him and that it fit the title of John's book; Good and Evil were weighted-out as if balanced in scale. The garden refers to our cemeteries we call Rose garden and the love affair with them. You can go out on a Sunday and will probably run into family members cleaning off grave markers or headstones, planting fresh flowers or having a toast to their loved ones.

In 1938 Sylvia Shaw Judson sculpted this statue, standing five feet tall and cast in bronze. She is one of six commissioned sculptures.

"The Birdgirl" was removed from the family plot in 1994 and is now on 'permanent loan' to the Telfair Museum. This beautiful little girl was left standing alone in a warehouse for a year and a half before finding her resting place at the Telfair in 1997.

The Telfair Museum is located at 121 Barnard Street, Telfair Square, Savannah, Georgia. If you visit the statue please remember that No Pictures are allowed inside as this is a museum.

Birdgirl statues ranging in a variety of sizes may be purchased from "The Book" Gift Shop (912) 233-3867 and can be shipped anywhere. For more information about "The Birdgirl" sculpture and Sylvia Shaw Judson, contact "The Book" Gift Shop to obtain the latest book by Sandra L. Underwood titled, *The "Bird Girl", The Story of a Sculpture by Sylvia Shaw Judson.*

CALENDAR OF EVENTS

JANUARY

First Saturday on Riverstreet — every month local arts and crafts; some entertainment.

Taste of Savannah — even writers from National Food Magazines come to this food event. For further information go to: www.tourismleadership.com

FEBRUARY

Georgia Day — February 12, 1733, Celebrate the founding of our Colony.

MARCH

St. Patrick's Day in Savannah — Celebrations abound and everything is green on March 17th and the week leading up to the BIG day, including the fountains, cocktails and the grits. Everyone is Irish on this special day filled with parties, a parade and more parties in the Squares after the parade.Come join the celebration, but book your reservations early.

Savannah Music Festival — 15 days of world class music, for more information go to: www.savannahmusicfestival.org

Annual Tour of Homes and Gardens — www.savannahtourofhomes.org.

APRIL

NOGS Tour of Hidden Gardens — www.savannahtourofhomes.org
Savannah Garden Expo - www.savannahgardenexpo.org

MAY

Savannah Seafood Festival — Sensational seafood from all over the Coastal Empire, live entertainment and loads of fun - www.savriverstreet.com

Savannah Shakespeare Festival — www.savannahga.gov

Scottish Games Festival — (912) 232-3945

JUNE

Savannah Asian Festival — www.savannahga.gov

JULY

Fourth of July Downtown Celebration — Fireworks on Riverstreet and other locations.

4th of July Beachside — Tybee Island celebration and fireworks.

AUGUST

Tybee Island Seafood and Music Festival — www.tybeevisit.com

SEPTEMBER

Savannah Jazz Festival — week long celebration of music with Jazz and Blues, www.coastaljazz.com

OCTOBER

Octoberfest — www.savriverstreet.com

Savannah Greek Festival — authentic food and merchandise - www.stpaul.ga.goarch.org

Savannah Film Festival — www.scad.edu

Jewish Food Festival & Hard Lox Café — 'Shalom Ya'll' - www.mickveisreal.org

NOVEMBER

Savannah Harbor Boat Parade of Lights — (912) 201-2201 - More than 60 festively decorated Yachts parade along the river.

DECEMBER

Christmas made in the South — Savannah Trade and Convention Center

Holiday Tour of Homes — What an event; a must see - www.dnaholidaytour.net

Christmas on the River — www.savriverstreet.com

Christmas in City Market — www.savannahcitymarket.com

Ideas for a "Midnight" Theme Party

Great for Card Club, Book Club, Fundraiser
Halloween or Christmas Party

Must serve Madera - Jim's favorite.

If you would rather serve a punch, may we suggest Chatham Artillery Punch or if something stronger is desired then try Pirates' House Punch or Pirates' House Skull Crusher. Please take responsibility for your guests (Joe would put them up for the night).

If using a "Midnight Punch" recipe, use an ice-ring. Pour bottled water in your favorite mold and drop 9 dimes (real or Dime Store plastic ones are fun) into mold and freeze. Right before party is to start, loosen from mold with warm water and place into punch bowl.

If your party is a nighttime party, use the theme "Moonlight and Magnolias." Use lots of candles, even place candles in every window, as if it were the holidays. Savannahians often do this for parties all year around.

Decorate with magnolias and greenery, use the "Birdgirl" statue and around the base place the greenery and big magnolias; some moss may even be appropriate. Small votive candles with wreaths in each of her bowls look lovely (just be careful with lighted candles). *If you do not have a "Birdgirl" statue, call "The Book" Gift Shop at (912) 233-3867 to place an order.*

Having a seated event; use small silk magnolias as napkin rings or decorate each chair with a big silk magnolia and some netting.

You must say *"Bless your heart"* at least a half dozen times throughout the party; a traditional Southern saying.

Music is a big part of the atmosphere; you must play "Emma" Lady of 6000 songs CD or one of her others. "The Book" Gift Shop carries all three of her CD's and may be ordered by calling (912) 233-3867.

Request Southern dress; seasonal hat and gloves for the ladies, coat, tie and handkerchief for the gentlemen.

Send your guest home with a *Thank You for coming Gift*. Make something or call "The Book" Gift Shop. We have bookmarks, pens, pencils, key chains, magnets, Midnight Cookie Tins and just about anything else you can think of regarding "Midnight" items.

As the host and/or hostess, it's your duty to see each guest out the door with their thank you gift, say good evening, wave to them as they get into their cars and keep waving until you can no longer see their tail lights; return, and start with the next departing guest.

Most of all have a great time with this and be creative. While some of these ideas may sound silly, they are really fun. Either we have done these ourselves or others have tried them and passed them along to us. Do not hesitate to take pictures of your event and email them to "The Book" Gift Shop. If you have questions or comments email these to us as well. Do not hesitate to order your items from us.

THE MAKING OF MIDNIGHT

THE TIME LINE

The Trials of Jim Williams

Jim Williams went through four trials for the slaying of Danny Lewis Hansford. This time line gives the progression from the slaying until Jim Williams death.

1981

May 2 - Danny Lewis Hansford, 21, shot by Williams at their home at 429 Bull Street. Williams says he was acting in self-defense. He is charged with murder and is released after posting a $25,000 bond; bond is later increased to $100,000.

July and August - Attorney Bobby Lee Cook of Summerville and Attorney John Wright Jones of Savannah form the defense team. Jones enters a plea of innocent for Williams August 12.

1982

January 26 - Trial number 1 opens.

January 29 - Jim Williams testifies in his own defense.

February 1 - Testimony is given that suggests that Williams and Hansford had a homosexual affair.

February 2 - Case goes to the jury of six men and six women. They deliberate four hours and return with a unanimous guilty verdict. Cook vows to appeal.

1983

January 5 - Georgia Supreme Court grants Williams a new trial. Attorney Cook had argued that inconsistencies in testimony by a Savannah police officer warranted overturning the conviction. The court ruled for a new trial "because we cannot and will not approve corruption of the truth-seeking function of the trial process." The court also blamed the prosecutors and not the judge for problems.

July 30 - Williams hires new lawyers. He is now to be represented by Savannah attorney Frank "Sonny" Seiler. He is to be assisted by

Atlanta lawyer Austin E. Catts and his law associate, Donald F. Samuel. The change was prompted by a trial conflict that had Bobby Lee Cook in federal court in Florida.

September 18 - The second trial begins.

September 26 - Fourteen jurors are selected. The jury of six men and six women is to be sequestered for the duration of the trial.

October 8 - Williams is convicted of murder and is sentenced to life in prison. The jury deliberated less than three hours before returning to court with the guilty verdict.

October 10 - Defense lawyers request appeal bond for Williams. Meanwhile, Williams is held in a medical cell away from the general inmate population in the Chatham County Jail. Sheriff Carl Griffin said it was done for "security reasons." Williams is later moved to a security cell with five other inmates.

November 3 - Judge George Oliver blocks the move of Williams into the state prison system while he appeals his murder conviction.

1984

January 4 - Williams blames news media for his conviction.

May 7 - Defense lawyers get postponement of a hearing of their new trial motion in the wake of new evidence that victim Danny Hansford may have tried to harm Williams. A new trial is requested.

May 29 - Yet another witness comes forward claiming Hansford planned to harm Williams.

May 31 - District attorney Spencer Lawton charges that the new witnesses for the defense were offered money.

August 16 - Williams is denied a new trial by Judge Oliver.

August 20 - Williams' lawyers plan to appeal to the Georgia Supreme Court for a new trial.

1985

February 4 - Arguments for a new trial are presented to the Georgia Supreme Court.

June 11 - The Georgia Supreme Court overturns the murder conviction of Williams and orders a new trial - his third.

June 13 - Williams seeks release on bond as he awaits his trial. He has been in jail since the October 8, 1983 conviction.

July 3 - Williams is granted a $250,000 bond and leaves the Chatham County Jail.

1986

April 14 - Lawyers Sonny Seiler and Don Samuel ask Judge Oliver to suppress evidence seized by police at Williams' home.

August 12 - In a pre-trial hearing, Williams testifies that he never gave police permission to search his home.

September 2 - Judge Oliver postpones Williams' retrial indefinitely.

1987

May 18 - Third trial starts.

May 26 - Three men and nine women are selected to hear case.

June 1 - Jim Williams describes how the killing happened.

June 5 - Jury begins deliberations.

June 9 - A lone juror holds out for acquittal. Judge Oliver declares a mistrial.

June 17 - Williams will get another trial and Judge James Head will preside.

1988

March 14 - Arguments are made by Williams' attorneys before the Georgia Supreme Court that a fourth trial for Williams would constitute double jeopardy.

May 26 - The Georgia Supreme Court rules that Lawton can try Williams a fourth time.

June 15 - The Georgia Supreme Court agrees to stay all action in Williams' trial for 90 days so that the defense can take its case to the U.S. Supreme Court.

October - The U.S. Supreme Court refuses to review the Williams' case, thereby allowing the fourth trial to happen.

1989

March 21 - Trial is moved to Augusta, Georgia. May 1 set as trial date.

May 3 - A jury of six men and six women is selected.

May 12 - After eight years, Jim Williams is acquitted of the murder of Danny Hansford.

1990

January 14 - James A. Williams, born December 11, 1930, is found dead at his home. An autopsy reveals that "some type of pneumonia" had killed him.

Bonaventure Cemetery

This garden of beauty sits less than 6 miles away from "The Book" Gift Shop. It is rich in history and is eternal home to some of the most interesting and famous characters in Savannah. With its setting on the Wilmington River in Thunderbolt, Georgia, one cannot help but be captivated by ornate statues, benches and gardens in all its splendor. Some of the most notables are the Trosdal family plot which once was home to the infamous "Bird Girl" statue; the Lawton family has some of the most beautiful statues in their section, and Savannah's native son, Johnny Mercer. If you have time, pack yourself a picnic basket and enjoy lunch and cocktail on the bench of Conrad Aiken, poet laureate. Whatever the occasion may be, take time to visit, but please be respectful, of those that have gone before us. And here's a warning, some of these spirits do not know they have passed on and may follow you home.

Directions from "The Book" Gift Shop:

Turn right onto Abercorn Street to East Victory Drive (Highway 80) - approximately 1.1 miles.

Turn left onto East Victory Drive (Highway 80 E) traveling approximately 4.07 miles until you see Downing Avenue (this will be to your left) - Landmarks are a sports bar on the left hand side and a Boat Dealer on your right.

Turn left onto Downing Avenue and upon reaching the end turn right onto Bonaventure Road.

After turning right onto Bonaventure Road, look for Bonaventure Cemetery on your left hand side.

Turn left through the gates then turn to your right to go to the old section. Also, there is an office located in the Bonaventure Cemetery so feel free to stop in and ask for a map of the area or directions.

A Little Story about Jim Williams

This story was given to us by a gentleman that came across Jim at an auction. It shows the lighter side of the business mogul, Jim Williams.

It happened one day in the 1970's that this young man, along with his father and mother, attended an auction at the Mount DeSales Catholic School, formerly a nunnery. Jim Williams placed a successful bid on a large safe, a very large safe. For some reason this safe was located on the second floor of the nunnery and had been enclosed by walls.

The terms of being the successful bidder meant the removal of the safe. Well, since the nunnery was going to be demolished, the walls surrounding the safe were going to be torn down anyway, so this would not pose a problem. Jim hired a crew, a large tow truck and a crane in order to have the safe moved from this location to his own. The nunnery was an old wooden building and there was no telling how long this 'monster of a safe' had been sitting there. In order to get the safe from the second floor onto the tow truck it would have to be moved from one side of the building to the other side where a large opening awaited with the crane's hoist chains. Jim's crew proceeded to use crowbars, rollers and ropes in order to make the safe easier to move. After a few hours of straining and groaning and heave-ho's, the men moved the safe ever so slowly across the floor toward the hole in the wall. As the men pulled the mighty safe into the middle of the room an eerie noise came from the floorboards under the safe. Suddenly, one of the crewmen yelled for everyone to get back! It was then and there that the flooring gave way to the weight of the mighty safe and there she went. First floor and no stopping her! The basement floor is where she came to rest and rest she did. The safe embedded itself into the basement floor a couple of feet, at least. To everyone's surprise there was not a single injury from the large safe's descent.

As for the rest of the story; after the dust had settled and everyone was cleared to be okay, Jim calmly walks over to the crater, looks down and as only Jim could say, 'damn, all that money spent on a crew, a truck and a crane has gone right through the floor.'

Needless to say, Jim found out why the safe was located in the strange place on the second floor. It was supported all those years by two huge concrete columns so once it was removed from its resting place over those columns the floor gave way.

Jim held up his end of the bargain and had the safe removed from the premises, but instead of lowering it down from the second floor he had it raised from the basement.

(Much thanks to the Thompson family for providing us with this little story)

"THE HAUNTED SAVANNAH"

Davenport © 1985 Sharon Saseen

HAUNTED PLACES

Haunted Places in Savannah

"The Book" Gift Shop   About one month after moving into the new location on Calhoun Square, Deborah called me about a problem in the back of "The Shop." She told me that she would smell smoke and that I needed to come down and see what was the problem. After going down to the shop I inspected the area in the back, referred to as the Jim Williams room, and even pulled up ceiling tiles, but I could not find any indication of something burning. After a couple of months of smelling smoke we received a phone call from the granddaughter of the local dentist that once lived in this home and occupied our shop as his dentist's office. She informed us that her grandparents rented out an apartment to an older lady that died in a fire in her apartment. The cause of the fire was later determined that the lady had fallen asleep while smoking in bed. Thus, we feel that the answer to the smelling of smoke is from the Lady that rented the apartment. We often tease each other in "The Shop" that 'Midnight' even intrigues the dead.

The Pirates House Restaurant reports spirits throughout, and not the kind you drink.

The Pink House Restaurant reports the ghost of James Habersham to still be roaming the halls, rearranging furniture and lighting candles.

The Hamilton - Turner Mansion (now a Bed & Breakfast), has young children still trapped upstairs and are full of mischief. Again, one of these happenings took place when Deborah was at the house and cleaning up after a party when she heard the sound of something rolling around upstairs. Knowing that no one else was in the house at the time she soon discovered a billiard ball rolling down the stairs. We knew the story with the children and figured it was them playing.

Moon River Brewing Company - even some of the local Haunted tour guides will no longer go into this building especially to the 2nd floor.

SAVANNAH—
MOST HAUNTED CITY IN USA

COBBLESTONE TOURS
(912) 604-3007
7pm to 9pm nightly - times are seasonal

GHOST TALK-GHOST WALK
(912) 233-3896 or (800) 563-3896

PLACES OF CURIOSITY

"The Book" Gift Shop - 'Most Haunted Merchandise' - located on Historic Calhoun Square, 127 East Gordon Street, (912) 233-3867. The shop has also witnessed sightings of an older grandmotherly-type woman. She has been a part of "The Shop's" history since 1997. Visitors, as well as spiritualists, have felt her presence and have mentioned this fact to the workers at the shop even before any of them were told about the ghost.

October 2004 was one of the strangest events. Upon opening the shop for business the owner heard the sound of running water and assumed the commode was the cause. When she discovered that this was not the problem a plumber was summonsed. His findings were most bizarre. The plumber discovered a hidden shower inside of a utility closet. The plumbing fixtures were behind a wooden wall, presumably put there by a previous owner. Upon tearing out this temporary wall, he found that one of the knobs was turned on to allow water to run from the showerhead. We can only assume that our *Ghost* was in need of a shower.

A photographer, Marty from Staunton, Virginia visited "The Shop" in November of 2005 and took various photos throughout. One particular photograph that he developed shows an 'orb' in one of the rooms. This photo is displayed in "The Book" Gift Shop and thus gives us further proof that something or someone is still watching over their domain.

Savannah Ghost Books to consider reading:

Savannah Specters - Margaret DeBolt

Savannah Ghost I & II - Al Cobb

Haunted Savannah - James Caskey

Danny's Bed - Al Cobb

Georgia Ghost - Nancy Roberts

Savannah Hauntings! - A walking guidebook
    by Robert Edgerly

All of the above books are available for purchase from "The Book" Gift Shop at (912) 233-3867.

FIRST...
IN SAVANNAH

The Savannah Cotton Exchange © 1996 Sharon Saseen

FACTS, ANSWERS
AND MAP

First...

- Capital of the 13th colony and later of Georgia, 1733
- City in North America planned on an extensive system of squares, 1734
- Agricultural experimental garden in North America, 1733
- Silk exportation in North America, 1735

- Moravian Church in North America, 1735
- Hymnal in Georgia, by John Wesley, 1736
- Lighthouse on South Atlantic coast, 1736
- Horserace in Georgia, 1740

- Cattle exportation in Georgia, 1755
- Newspaper in the colony, Georgia Gazette, 1763
- Negro Baptist congregation in U.S., 1788
- Public school in Georgia, 1788
- Practical cotton gin, Eli Whitney, 1793

- Steamship to cross an ocean, the S.S. Savannah, 1819
- Hospital for Negroes in U.S., Georgia Infirmary, 1832
- Commercially successful iron steamship, the S.S. John Randolph, 1834
- Use of rifled cannon in modern warfare, at Fort Pulaski, 1862

- Motorized fire department in U.S., 1911
- Girl Scout troop, founded by Juliette Gordon Low, 1912
- Nuclear-powered merchant ship, the N.S. Savannah, 1962
- Garden for the Blind in the Southeast, 1963

MIDNIGHT TRIVIA ANSWERS

1. May 2, 1981
2. Jim Williams purchased a jade Faberge box that cost him $70,000.
3. Four
4. The flea collar and the no-pest strip
5. A red brick
6. Psycho Dice
7. 16; One must be married
8. Started in 1893, it was a means of entertainment for ladies while their husbands worked
9. Cosmo Mariner, Destination Unknown
10. And the Angels Sing
11. A big tombstone; No
12. She pats the tomato slices with a paper towel so the sandwiches are never soggy
13. Sadie Jefferson
14. Rum-drinking pirates (Treasure Island); Strong-willed women (Gone With the Wind and Sadie Jefferson); Courtly manners (Gone With the Wind); Eccentric behavior (Sadie Jefferson); Gentle words (just the name - Savannah); Lovely music (Johnny Mercer)
15. "A beautiful woman with a dirty face"
16. The University of Georgia mascots
17. The Pickup
18. Four
19. Johnny Mercer's nephew introduced them over the telephone
20. Helen Drexel
21. Maurice Tempelsman
22. Four
23. Purple-tinted, wire-rimmed glasses
24. Chablis
25. Danny could pick up enough speed so that when he hit the swayback bump all four wheels of his car would come off the road.
26. Moe Fetzer
27. B-E-D-R-O-O-M
28. Charleston, South Carolina
29. The assassination of Abraham Lincoln
30. Glory
31. Marilyn Case testified that Danny Hansford's hands were not bagged when his body was brought to the hospital; She wrapped them in plastic when she should have used paper
32. Bobby Lee Cook
33. Bobby Lee Cook was from the mountains of Summerville, Ga. He believed that a local jury would not trust an out-of-town lawyer.
34. Her pay envelope was $100 short
35. A silver shaker of mixed martinis, 2 silver goblets and 2 linen napkins
36. Clint Eastwood
37. Wanda would usually bump into folks causing them to spill their drinks. What else could they do but buy another
38. New York
39. Nine shiny dimes and "fresh water that ain't run through no pipe" The water had to be in a quart jar with no label on it
40. Lottery numbers
41. King Edward cigarillos
42. A black Camaro
43. Augusta, Georgia
44. Pirating electricity from his neighbor

45. Prince Charles
46. Green, including her fingernails and toe nails
47. An "in-stack" the "out-stack" and sometimes the wastepaper basket
48. Patrick, the dog, had died; however, Mr. Glover continued his walks with Patrick so that he would continue to receive a salary from his late employer's (Mr. Bouhan, not Patrick) estate.
49. Jack Leigh
50. A false step and a front door that doubles as a cooling board
51. Chablis called him with the news
52. (1) Always stick around for another drink (2) Never go South of Gaston Street (3) Observe the high-holidays; St. Patrick's Day and the day of the Georgia-Florida football game. Joe broke rule #2
53. 24; 21
54. Because the Oglethorpe Club would not allow her daughter, who was a police officer, to wear trousers to the club
55. George Mercer, III; "George, you drink too much"
56. General James Oglethorpe
57. The Jewels of Savannah
58. Stormy Weather
59. Architectural Digest
60. Twenty one
61. Dr. Joseph Burton; He was working on the child murder case of Wayne Williams
62. Hypoglycemia
63. Esquire; he served as editor for New York Magazine
64. Bruce Kelly, Ga landscape architect
65. She was listed as a defense witness
66. Hamilton-Turner House

67. His heavy black shoes with thick rubber soles
68. Palm Trees
69. Emma Kelly
70. Sweet Georgia Browns
71. Candlelight seen through the windows of the Mercer House
72. Eggs, bacon, a bayer aspirin, and a glass of spirits of ammonia and a coco-cola
73. The Georgia Gazette
74. Gordon, Georgia
75. Because his employee wore purple eye-shadow over one eye
76. A Disturbed Jennifer; It was a rouge group made up of 4 green-haired SCAD students
77. A Pod; 20x20; 8 inmates
78. Gaston's Tomb aka a Stranger's Tomb; this is where someone would be kept if they happened to die while visiting Savannah, until arrangements could be made
79. Jim had scheduled a buying trip to England
80. The Trosdal
81. Sentimental Gentleman
82. $18,000
83. He was his barber
84. Guilty, released on Bond
85. Spencer Lawton
86. Clary's
87. Moon River, Wine & Roses, Accentuate the Positive (there are many)
88. A view from Pompey's Head
89. Funeral expenses
90. Serena Dawes
91. Mr. Bouhan
92. Jane Wright
93. Lunch from Mrs. Wilkes, dinner from Johnny Harris one night and dinner at Elizabeth's the next night
94. 15 minutes; Not Guilty
95. Goldfish

MAP KEY FOR
"MIDNIGHT" SITES OF INTEREST

❶ Mercer House
429 Bull Street
Splendid Italianate mansion of main character Jim Williams; it is considered one of the finest homes in Savannah. Well known for extravagant parties and unfortunate tragedies. It is located on the southwest corner of Monterey Square.

❷ Congregation Mickve Israel
20 E. Gordon Street
Established in 1733, it is the oldest congregation of Reform Judaism in the United States. Located directly across Monterey Square from Mercer House, its members were the most shocked when Jim Williams unfurled the Nazi banner on "Flag Day."

❸ Serena Dawes Home
17 W. Gordon Street
Considered one of the most beautiful women in the world, Serena Dawes is a pseudonym for the late Helen Drexel. Well known for her eccentricities, she was often said to "hold court" in her boudoir rather than the parlor.

❹ The Oglethorpe Club
450 Bull Street
Only the crème de la crème grace the doors of this exclusive club. But ladies be forewarned: if you don't wear a dress, you can't come in.

❺ Williams Antique Shop
430 Whitaker Street
The finest antiques in the world could be discovered in the detached carriage house of Jim Williams. No longer an antique shop, it is now a private residence.

❻ 16 E. Jones Street
Former "rental" property of the notorious Joe Odom. If you were looking for a good party at any hour of the night, this was the place to be.

❼ 22 E. Jones Street
After several visits to Savannah, author John Berendt took up residence in the carriage house of this East Jones Street townhouse to gather more information for *Midnight in the Garden of Good and Evil.*

❽ Joe Odom's Third Residence
128 W. Harris Street
Reputedly, while the owners were in Europe, Joe took up unauthorized residence at this beautiful home. Actually, he did pay rent, his checks just bounced.

❾ Hamilton-Turner House
330 Abercorn Street
Fourth home of Joe Odom. It is now the residence of the buxom blonde, former Miss BBW "Mandy Nichols", aka Nancy Hillis. Tours of the house are given daily. The former Sweet Georgia Brown's chanteuse also has B&B accommodations, etc.

❿ Clary's Drug Store
402 Abercorn Street
No longer an apothecary, Clary's is still a favorite eatery for locals in downtown Savannah. A frequent haunt of "Luther Driggers" and many others.

⓫ Lady Chablis's Former Residence
Often overlooked, Crawford Square is one of Savannah's 0most charming sites. The Lady Chablis was lucky enough to have an apartment on Houston Street between E. McDonough Street and E. Perry Street.

⓬ Chatham County Courthouse
133 Montgomery Street
Location of three of Jim William's trials for the murder of Danny Hansford.

⓭ Conrad Aiken Homes
228 and 230 E. Oglethorpe Avenue
Pulitzer Prize winning author and poet, he sadly overheard the events leading to is parent's violent murder-suicide deaths. Years later he returned to Savannah and took up residence in the home directly next door. He was well known locally for his daily "cocktail hour" practices.

⓮ Club One
1 Jefferson Street
The Lady Chablis frequently preformed at this popular Savannah nightspot. When her schedule allows, you may still be lucky enough to see her strut her stuff. Call 232-0200 for more information.

⓯ Bonaventure Cemetery
Located on the banks of the Wilmington River, Bonaventure Cemetery is a lush sanctuary lined with oak trees, where many of Savannah's most prominent citizens are entombed, including Conrad Aiken, plot H-48. Danny Hansford is buried in **Greenwich Cemetery**, next to Bonaventure, in section 8, row G, lot 6. About four miles east of downtown Savannah, take E. Liberty Street until it becomes Skidaway Road, then turn left at Bonaventure Road.

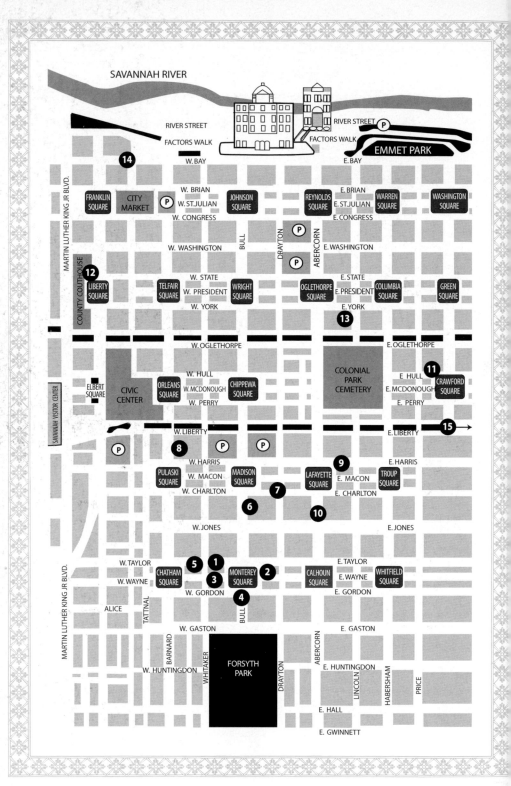

SAVANNAH RIVER

RIVER STREET

FACTORS WALK

W. BAY

RIVER STREET

FACTORS WALK

E. BAY

EMMET PARK

14

FRANKLIN SQUARE

CITY MARKET

W. BRIAN

W. ST.JULIAN

W. CONGRESS

JOHNSON SQUARE

E. BRIAN

E. ST.JULIAN

E. CONGRESS

REYNOLDS SQUARE

WARREN SQUARE

WASHINGTON SQUARE

W. WASHINGTON

BULL

DRAYTON

ABERCORN

E. WASHINGTON

MARTIN LUTHER KING JR BLVD.

COUNTY COURTHOUSE

12

LIBERTY SQUARE

TELFAIR SQUARE

W. STATE

W. PRESIDENT

W. YORK

WRIGHT SQUARE

OGLETHORPE SQUARE

E. STATE

E. PRESIDENT

E. YORK

COLUMBIA SQUARE

GREEN SQUARE

13

W. OGLETHORPE

E. OGLETHORPE

ELBERT SQUARE

CIVIC CENTER

ORLEANS SQUARE

W. HULL

W.McDONOUGH

W. PERRY

CHIPPEWA SQUARE

COLONIAL PARK CEMETERY

E Hull

E.McDONOUGH

E. PERRY

11

CRAWFORD SQUARE

SAVANNAH VISITOR CENTER

W. LIBERTY

E. LIBERTY

15

8

PULASKI SQUARE

W. HARRIS

W. MACON

W. CHARLTON

MADISON SQUARE

LAFAYETTE SQUARE

9

E. HARRIS

E. MACON

E. CHARLTON

TROUP SQUARE

7

6

10

W. JONES

E. JONES

W. TAYLOR

5 **1**

CHATHAM SQUARE

3

W. WAYNE

W. GORDON

MONTEREY SQUARE

2

4

E. TAYLOR

CALHOUN SQUARE

E. WAYNE

E. GORDON

WHITFIELD SQUARE

ALICE

TATTNAL

BULL

MARTIN LUTHER KING JR BLVD.

BARNARD

WHITAKER

W. GASTON

FORSYTH PARK

DRAYTON

ABERCORN

E. GASTON

LINCOLN

HABERSHAM

PRICE

W. HUNTINGDON

E. HUNTINGDON

E. HALL

E. GWINNETT

INDEX

Andrew Low House © Sharon Saseen

The Restaurants

Index

Tips:

Butter or Margarine

1 stick . . . . 4 ounces or ¼ pound
2 sticks . . . . 8 ounces or ½ pound
3 sticks . . . . 12 ounces or ¾ pound
4 sticks . . . . 16 ounces or 1 pound

¼ cup . . . . 2 ounces or ½ stick
½ cup . . . . 4 ounces or 1 stick
¾ cup . . . . 6 ounces or 1 ½ sticks
1 cup . . . . 8 ounces or 2 sticks

A pinch . . . . 1/8 teaspoon or less
3 teaspoons . . . . 1 tablespoon
4 tablespoons . . . . ¼ cup
8 tablespoons . . . . ½ cup
12 tablespoons . . . . ¾ cup
16 tablespoons . . . . 1 cup
2 cups . . . . 1 pint
4 cups . . . . 1 quart
4 quarts . . . . 1 gallon
16 ounces . . . . 1 pound
32 quarts . . . . 1 quart
1 ounce liquid . . . . 2 tablespoons
8 ounces liquid. . . . . 1 cup

Double boiler - No need to go out and buy one. Place a heat-proof bowl in a skillet full of water; then you will have your own double boiler.

Vidalia Onions - These are sweet onions born then raised on farms in Vidalia, Georgia. We prefer using these, not because they are so readily available to us, but they are great. If you cannot find these in your area, use your favorite brand.